LEFT

BIBLE STUD

BEH

The Rapture

Neil Wilson and Len Woods

MOODY PUBLISHERS

CHICAGO

Written by Neil Wilson and Len Woods.

Produced with the assistance of the Livingstone Corporation (www.LivingstoneCorp.com). Project staff includes Len Woods, Neil Wilson, Ashley Taylor, Kirk Luttrell, Mary Horner Collins, Mark Wainwright, Carol Barnstable, and Rosalie Krusemark.

ISBN 0-8024-6465-3

1 3 5 7 9 10 8 6 4 2

Printed in the United States of America

Contents

Foreword by Tim LaHaye and Jerry B. Jenkins 5

Introduction 6

How to Get the Most from Your Study 7

Leading a Group Through the Left Behind Studies 8

How to Study Bible Prophecy (by Tim LaHaye) 10

Rapture Overview 12

    Lesson 1: Early Edition (How Biblical Prophecy Works) 13

    Lesson 2: Instant Exit 27

    Lesson 3: The Big Picture 41

    Lesson 4: One Coming—Two Phases 55

    Lesson 5: Aftermath 69

    Lesson 6: Don't Be Left Behind 81

Endnotes 95

For the latest information on other Left Behind series and Bible prophecy products, go to www.leftbehind.com. Sign up for a free e-mail update!

Foreword

Tim LaHaye and Jerry B. Jenkins

Jesus said, "Watch and wait!" (Mark 13:32–37).

Even believers looking for the coming of Christ will be surprised at the Rapture. But it will be a delightful surprise—the fulfillment of our deepest longings. One of our goals in the Left Behind novels is to keep others from being surprised in the worst sense—by being caught off guard and left behind.

A large body of literature written in the last half century highlights the growing evidence that Christ's coming is quickly drawing near. We have written several books ourselves seeking to help people understand biblical passages about the end times. *Are We Living in the End Times?* (Tyndale), *The Tim LaHaye Prophecy Study Bible* (AMG), *Will I Be Left Behind?* (Tyndale), and *Perhaps Today* (Tyndale) all were written to help people understand biblical prophecy.

The Left Behind Bible study guide series from Moody Publishers uses material from the novels to illustrate an introduction to Bible prophecy. Authors Neil Wilson and Len Woods emphasize that the Left Behind stories are rooted in biblical themes. They bring together various prophetic passages of Scripture and plenty of thought-provoking questions, with the goal of getting you to live in the light of the imminent return of Christ.

These studies will help you discover what we wanted to show in the novels—that all the historical, technological, and theological pieces of the puzzle recorded in biblical prophecy are more plainly in place for Christ's return now than ever before. Technological advances commonplace today parallel scriptural pictures in such an uncanny way that they allow for prophesied events that even a generation ago seemed impossible.

Biblical prophecy doesn't look nearly as strange anymore. Our intent in the novels was to simply make the truth of the Bible come alive for fiction readers. That many people have been driven back to their Bibles is a wonderful outcome. In your hands is another vehicle that allows you to closely study the Bible texts that thrilled us and served as the basis for the fiction. We encourage you to become a wise student of God's Word and a watchful observer of the times.

Introduction

Neil Wilson and Len Woods

Welcome to this introductory study of end-times prophecy! We pray that you will find these studies helpful, challenging, and encouraging in your walk with Christ.

General interest in prophecy among Christians tends to behave very much like an active volcano. About once in each generation, seismic events in history grab everyone's attention, and the internal pressure to see events from God's point of view causes an eruption of prophetic concerns. Early in our generation toward the end of the 1960s, we experienced just such an eruption with the turbulence surrounding the Vietnam conflict, the heating up of the Cold War, the rise of the Jesus Movement, and the publication of Hal Lindsay's book *The Late Great Planet Earth,* among other things. Larry Norman's song "I Wish We'd All Been Ready" struck a chord of longing and urged our generation to get serious about Jesus. He was coming like a thief in the night. Prophetic students pointed to the rebirth of the nation of Israel and the rapidly closing time period following that event as an indisputable clue to Christ's coming. We tried to get ready—for a while.

Unfortunately, like many examples of public fascination, the wide interest in prophetic issues gradually dwindled to the faithful remnant, who continually read the signs of the times and served the body of Christ with urgent warnings. The volcano seemed to go silent. Here and there, prophecy conferences still gathered. Books were written, papers presented, and even heated arguments raged behind closed doors. The world quickly went on its way to more hopeful outlooks: the fall of the Berlin Wall, the explosive rise of the stock market, and murmured promises that the world might finally be headed toward life as a kinder, gentler place. Continual background trouble was ignored. Even the body of Christ seemed fascinated with herself. The potential of church growth achieved by appealing to seekers and making it very easy to slide into the church created an atmosphere where judgment and Christ's second coming sounded a little harsh and unfriendly. The church became, in many ways, too successful to long for rapture. The distant rumble of the volcano was drowned out by the music of worship that too often sounded a lot more like entertainment than serious consideration of the majesty of God.

The arrival of new centuries and the much rarer dawn of new millenniums have usually created a suspicion that more than just a calendar time line might be coming to an end. Recently, terms like Y2K became shorthand for fearful brooding over the sudden realization that our entire civilization seemed dependent on countless computers remaining sane in spite of a simple change in their internal clocks. Many expected a cyber meltdown. Some predicted a new Dark Ages. Thousands stockpiled food, water, and guns. And most of us wondered what would happen. Christians who knew prophecy simply couldn't see cataclysmic Y2K scenarios indicated in the Bible. Their more or less confident counsel to trust in God's sovereignty was often met with suspicion and derision by those practical believers, whose motto seemed to be "God helps those who help themselves." Y2K caught the church unprepared.

In the predawn jitters of the new millennium, a book was published that seemed to almost instantly grab the imagination of millions. *Left Behind* became plausible fiction. As Tim LaHaye and Jerry Jenkins have repeatedly stated, one of their primary goals was to demonstrate that all the technology was already in place to allow prophetic events to occur that previous generations had found inconceivable. A volcano of interest in prophecy began to rumble. The tremors found their way to the shelves of the largest general market bookstores as millions of *Left Behind* books left the stores. Many Christians reported surprise over their own lack of understanding of what seems so apparent throughout Scripture. In the years that have followed the publication of the first novel, there has been a healthy movement toward greater acknowledgment that God has a plan for this world, and a deadline is approaching. His Word makes that fact clear, and the events of history are providing confirming echoes.

We trust these studies will tune your heart and mind to the purposes of God. We hope that as a result of studying his Word, you will long for your daily life to harmonize with God's purposes. We pray that you increasingly will be intent on doing what God has set before you, glancing from time to time at the horizon, anticipating your personal encounter with the Lord! May your prayers frequently include, "Maranatha!"—Lord, come quickly!

How to Get the Most from Your Study

Depending on your background and experiences, the Left Behind studies will

- Help you begin to answer some important questions that may have occurred to you as you were reading the Left Behind novels,
- Introduce you to the serious study of biblical prophecy,
- Provide you with a starting point for a personal review of biblical prophecy that you remember hearing about as you were growing up, or
- Offer you a format to use in meeting with others to discuss not only the Left Behind novels but also the Bible texts that inspired the stories.

If you are using these studies on your own, you will establish your own pace. A thoughtful consideration of the Bible passages, questions, and quotes from the Left Behind series and other books will require a minimum of an hour for each lesson.

If you will be discussing these lessons as part of a group, make sure you review each lesson on your own. Your efforts in preparation will result in a number of personal benefits:

- You will have thought through some of the most important questions and be less prone to "shallow answers."

- You will have a good sense of the direction of the discussion.

- You will have an opportunity to do some added research if you discover an area or question that you know will be beyond the scope of the group discussion.

- Since a group will probably not be able to cover every question in each lesson because of time constraints, your preparation will allow you to fill in the gaps.

Tools to Use

- Make sure you have a Bible you can read easily.

- Most of the quotes in these studies come from the New Living Translation. If your Bible is a different version, get in the habit of comparing the verses.

- Consider reading some of the excellent books available today for the study of prophecy. You will find helpful suggestions in the endnotes.

- Put some mileage on your pen or pencil. Take time to write out answers to the questions as you prepare each lesson.

- Continually place your life before God. Ultimately, your study of prophecy ought to deepen your awareness of both his sovereignty and compassion. You will appreciate the overwhelming aspects of God's love, mercy, and grace toward you even more as you get a wider view of his grandeur and glory.

Leading a Group Through the Left Behind Studies

Leading a Bible study on prophecy can be daunting to any teacher. When it comes to prophecy, all of us are students; we've all got a lot to learn. Approaching this study as a fresh opportunity to ask questions, to seek the Lord and his Word for answers, and to help others in the process will take the burden of being "the teacher" off your shoulders.

Remember that it's helpful to be confident in what you know as long as you're not confident you know everything. The study of prophecy does bring up many questions for which the most honest answer is, "We don't know." God has, however, given us more information in his Word than he is often given credit for. To use the apostle Paul's language, we may see some things sharply and other things dimly, but that's so much better than being in the dark. Take a careful look at Tim LaHaye's article "How to Study Prophecy," and encourage your group to read it. It provides valuable guidelines as you prepare for these discussions.

No matter the level of knowledge you or your group may have, set your sights on increasing your group's interest in the study of prophecy as well as deepening their commitment to living for Christ. Keep your group focused on the need to know Jesus better. Ultimately, it's hard to get excited about expecting a stranger. The more intimately we get to know Jesus, the more we long to see him. Consider using as a motto for your group the words of Paul, "Yet I am not ashamed, because I know whom I have believed, and am convinced that he is able to guard what I have entrusted to him for that day" (2 Timothy 1:12 NIV).

Prophecy and evangelism travel together. A study like this can provide unexpected opportunities to share the gospel. We tend to think that evangelistic conversations are primarily a backward look with a present application—God has accomplished certain gracious things through Christ and his death and resurrection; therefore, what shall we do today? Prophecy reverses the discussion, creating a forward look with a present application—God promises he will do these things tomorrow; therefore, how shall we live today? Be prayerfully alert to opportunities during and after studies to interact seriously with group members about the state of their souls. Tim LaHaye and Jerry Jenkins have letters from hundreds of readers of the Left Behind series who came to faith in Christ in part as a result of their exposure to prophecy. Pray that God will use your study to accomplish his purposes in others' lives, including yours.

Several Helpful Tools

Bibles: Encourage group members to bring and use their Bibles. We've quoted in the workbook the verses being discussed in each lesson, but having the full context of the verses available to examine is often helpful. We recommend that you have on hand for consultation at least one copy of a trustworthy study Bible that highlights prophetic issues, such as the *Ryrie Study Bible* (Moody Press) or the *Tim LaHaye Prophecy Study Bible* (AMG Publishers).

Bible Concordance and Bible Dictionary: Each of these tools can assist a group in the process of finding specific passages in Scripture or gaining a perspective on a particular biblical theme or word.

Resource Books: The endnotes for each lesson include a number of books from which insightful quotes have been drawn. If members in your group have access to these books, encourage them to make the volumes available for others to read.

Left Behind Novels: Because there are several editions of the books, you may discover some discrepancies in the page listings of the quotes from the novels and the particular books you have. A little search of the pages nearby will usually get you to the right place.

Hints for Group Sessions

1. Encourage participants to review and prepare as much of each lesson as they are able in advance. Remind them it will help the learning process if they have been thinking about the issues and subjects before the session.
2. As you prepare the lessons, decide what questions you will make your focus for discussion. Unless your time is open-ended and your group highly motivated, you will not be able to cover every question adequately in an hour.
3. Only experience with your particular group will give you a sense of how much ground you can cover each session.
4. Consider appointing different group members to ask the questions. That will take the spotlight off you and allow them to participate in a comfortable way.
5. Take time in each session for feedback and questions from the group. These spontaneous reflections will give you a good sense of how much the group is learning, integrating, and being affected by the lessons.

The Place of Prayer

Make it a point to pray with the group and for the group during the study. Use part of your preparation time to bring each person from the group before God in prayer. Open and close each session by asking God, who alone knows the full meaning of every prophecy he has inspired in his Word, to open your hearts and minds to understand and respond in practical, wholehearted ways to the truth of Scripture.

How to Study Bible Prophecy

Tim LaHaye

Prophecy is God's road map to show us where history is going. The Bible's predictions claim literal and specific fulfillments that verify that such prophecies are indeed from God. The key to interpreting Bible prophecy is in discerning what is literal and what is symbolic. Therefore, the best way to avoid confusion in the study of prophetic Scripture is to follow these simple directions:

1. Interpret prophecy literally wherever possible. God meant what he said and said what he meant when he inspired "holy men of God [who] spake as they were moved by the Holy Ghost" (2 Peter 1:21 KJV) to write the Bible. Consequently we can take the Bible literally most of the time. Where God intends for us to interpret symbolically, he makes it obvious.

One of the reasons the book of Revelation is difficult for some people to understand is that they try to spiritualize the symbols used in the book. However, since many Old Testament prophecies have already been literally fulfilled, such as God turning water to blood (Exodus 4:9; 7:17–21), it should not be difficult to imagine that future prophetic events can and will be literally fulfilled at the appropriate time. Only when symbols or figures of speech make absolutely no literal sense should anything but a literal interpretation be sought.

2. Prophecies concerning Israel and the church should not be transposed. The promises of God to Israel to be fulfilled "in the latter days," particularly those concerning Israel's punishment during the Tribulation, have absolutely nothing to do with the church. The Bible gives specific promises for the church that she will be raptured into heaven before the Tribulation (John 14:2–3; 1 Corinthians 15:51–52; 1 Thessalonians 4:13–18).

3. For symbolic passages, compare Scripture with Scripture. The Bible is not contradictory. Even though written by numerous divinely inspired men over a period of sixteen hundred years, it is supernaturally consistent in its use of terms. For example, the word "beast" is used thirty-four times in Revelation and many other times in Scripture. Daniel explains that the word is symbolic of either a king or kingdom (see Daniel 7–8). By examining the contexts in Revelation and Daniel, you will find that "beast" has the same meaning in both books. Many other symbols used in Revelation are also taken directly from the Old Testament. These include "the tree of life" (Revelation 2:7; 22:2, 14), "the Book of Life" (Revelation 3:5), and Babylon (Revelation 14:8ff.).

Some symbols in Revelation are drawn from other New Testament passages. These include terms such as "the word of God" (1:2, 9ff.), "Son of Man" (1:13; 14:14), "marriage supper" (19:9), "the bride" (21:9; 22:17), "first resurrection" (20:5–6), and "second death" (2:11; 20:6, 14; 21:8). Other symbols in Revelation are explained and identified in their context. For example, "Alpha and Omega" represents Jesus Christ (1:8; 21:6; 22:13); the "seven candlesticks" (1:13, 20) are the seven churches; the "dragon" is Satan (12:3ff.); and the "man child" is Jesus (12:5, 13).

Though some prophetic passages should be interpreted symbolically, it is important to remember that symbols in the Bible depict real people, things, and events. For example, the "seven candlesticks" in Revelation 1 represent real churches that actually existed when the prophecy was given.

Keeping the three points above in mind will provide you with a confident approach to prophetic Scriptures and guard against a multitude of errors. Allow God's Word always to be your final guide.

(Adapted from the *Tim LaHaye Prophecy Study Bible*, AMG Publishers, used with permission.)

Overview of the End Times

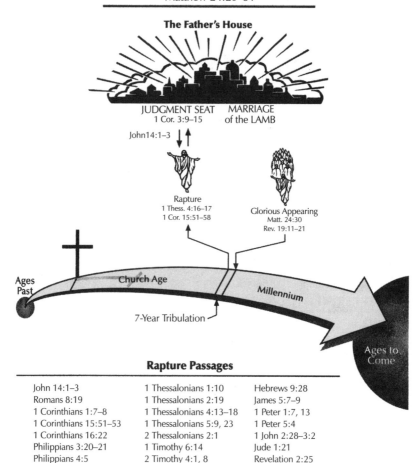

End-Times Overview
Matthew 24:29–31

The Father's House

JUDGMENT SEAT MARRIAGE
1 Cor. 3:9–15 of the LAMB

John14:1–3

Rapture
1 Thess. 4:16–17
1 Cor. 15:51–58

Glorious Appearing
Matt. 24:30
Rev. 19:11–21

Ages
Past

Church Age

Millennium

7-Year Tribulation

Ages to
Come

Rapture Passages

John 14:1–3	1 Thessalonians 1:10	Hebrews 9:28
Romans 8:19	1 Thessalonians 2:19	James 5:7–9
1 Corinthians 1:7–8	1 Thessalonians 4:13–18	1 Peter 1:7, 13
1 Corinthians 15:51–53	1 Thessalonians 5:9, 23	1 Peter 5:4
1 Corinthians 16:22	2 Thessalonians 2:1	1 John 2:28–3:2
Philippians 3:20–21	1 Timothy 6:14	Jude 1:21
Philippians 4:5	2 Timothy 4:1, 8	Revelation 2:25
Colossians 3:4	Titus 2:13	Revelation 3:10

Second Coming Passages

Daniel 2:44–45	Mark 13:14–27	1 Peter 4:12–13
Daniel 7:9–14	Mark 14:62	2 Peter 3:1–14
Daniel 12:1–3	Luke 21:25–28	Jude 1:14–15
Zechariah 12:10	Acts 1:9–11	Revelation 1:7
Zechariah 14:1–15	Acts 3:19–21	Revelation 19:11–20:6
Matthew 13:41	1 Thessalonians 3:13	Revelation 22:7, 12, 20
Matthew 24:15–31	2 Thessalonians 1:6–10	
Matthew 26:64	2 Thessalonians 2:8	

LEFT

BIBLE STUDY GUIDE #1

BEHIND

The Rapture

Lesson 1
Early Edition (How Biblical Prophecy Works)

1. Why are so many people fascinated with the future?

_____

_____

_____

_____

2. What are some methods people use to try to see into the future? In your opinion what makes books like *Left Behind* so popular with readers?

_____

_____

_____

_____

_____

3. If you have read the Left Behind books, which one is your favorite, and why?

_____

_____

_____

_____

4. What in the books has made the biggest impression on you? Is your life different as a result? In what way?

_____

_____

_____

_____

_____

Unfolding the Story

(*Left Behind*, pp. 121–23)

The first book of the Left Behind series begins with the sudden disappearance (i.e., the Rapture) of all Christians everywhere. Those not caught up to meet Christ in the air (i.e., unbelievers) are left on the earth to try to make heads or tails of this cataclysmic event.

One of the main characters in the novels, an airline pilot named Rayford Steele, is not a believer in Jesus Christ. He has been left behind. Understandably, he is mourning the disappearance of his wife and son and more than a little concerned about the fate of his daughter and himself. Rayford's wife had been a devout Christian who had tried repeatedly to talk to her stubborn husband about the Bible and the need for faith in Christ. He hadn't listened.

RAYFORD STEELE LAY ON HIS BACK, staring at the ceiling. Sleep had come hard and intermittently, and he hated the logy feeling. He didn't want to watch the news. He didn't want to read the paper, even knowing a new one had flopped up onto the porch before dawn. All he wanted was for Chloe to get home so they could grieve together. There was nothing, he decided, more lonely than grief.

He and his daughter would have work to do, too. He wanted to investigate, to learn, to know, to act. He started by searching for a Bible, not the family Bible that had collected dust on his shelf for years, but Irene's. Hers would have notes in that, maybe something that would point him in the right direction.

It wasn't hard to find. It was usually within arm's reach of where she slept. He found it on the floor, next to the bed. Would there be some guide? An index? Something that referred to the Rapture or the judgment or something? If not, maybe he'd start at the end. If genesis meant "beginning," maybe revelation had something to do with the end, even though it didn't mean that. The only Bible verse Rayford could quote by heart was Genesis 1:1: "In the beginning God created the heavens and the earth." He hoped there'd be some corresponding verse at the end of the Bible that said something like, "In the end God took all his people to heaven and gave everybody else one more chance."

But no such luck. The very last verse in the Bible meant nothing to him. It said, "The grace of the Lord Jesus be with you all. Amen." And it sounded like the religious mumbo jumbo he had heard in church. He backed up a verse and read, "He who testifies to these things says, 'Yes, I am coming quickly.' Amen. Come, Lord Jesus."

Now he was getting somewhere. Who was this who testified of these things, and what were these things? The quoted words were in red. What did that mean? He looked through the Bible and then noticed on the spine, "Words of Christ in Red." So Jesus said he was coming quickly. Had he come? And if the Bible was as old as it seemed, what did "quickly" mean? It must have meant soon, unless it was from the perspective of someone with a long view of history. Maybe Jesus meant that when he came, he would do it quickly. Was that what this was all about? Rayford glanced at the last chapter as a whole. Three other verses had red letters, and two of those repeated the business about coming quickly.

Rayford could make no sense of the text of the chapter. It seemed old and formal. But near the end of the chapter was a verse that ended with words that had a strange impact on him. Without a hint of their meaning, he read, "Let the one who is thirsty come; let the one who wishes take the water of life without cost."

Jesus wouldn't have been the one who was thirsty. He would not have been the one who wished to take the water of life. That, Rayford assumed, referred to the reader. It struck him that he was thirsty, soul thirsty. But what was the water of life? He had already paid a terrible cost for missing it. Whatever it was, it had been in this book for hundreds of years.

Rayford idly leafed through the Bible to other passages, none of which made sense to him. They discouraged him because they didn't seem to flow together, to refer to each other, to have a direction. Language and concepts foreign to him were not helping.

5. Why do you think Rayford opted for his wife's Bible and not the big family Bible on the living room shelf?

_____

_____

_____

6. Why do you think he went looking for help and answers in the book of Revelation?

_____

_____

_____

_____

Back to Reality

Rayford wasn't alone in his confusion, in his inability to understand the Bible. Most people, including a high percentage of Christians, don't have a clue how to make sense of the Bible, especially the parts of the Bible that concern future things.

7. What would you say are the primary reasons the average person doesn't know more about the Bible?

_____

_____

_____

_____

8. What keeps people (especially those who claim to be followers of Christ) from reading and studying the Bible?

_____

_____

_____

_____

_____

9. On a scale of 1–10 (with 1 meaning "total cluelessness" and 10 meaning "absolute comprehension"), how would you rate your own understanding of what the Bible says about the end times?

_____

_____

_____

In his classic work *Living by the Book,* Dr. Howard Hendricks lists a number of reasons people give for *not* reading the Bible:

- ☐ The Bible doesn't seem relevant to my life.
- ☐ The Bible seems confusing and hard to understand. I don't know how to make sense of it.
- ☐ I used to read the Bible, and it made me feel good. But after a while, it didn't seem to have the same impact, so finally I gave it up.
- ☐ I feel guilty when I read the Bible.
- ☐ The Bible is hopelessly out-of-date. It may have some interesting stories, but it has little significance for life today.
- ☐ I rely on my pastor or minister to explain the Bible to me. If I need to know something, he will tell me about it.
- ☐ I have doubts about the Bible's reliability.
- ☐ I don't have time. I'm just too busy.
- ☐ The Bible seems boring to me.
- ☐ I don't own a Bible.
- ☐ The Bible is full of myths and half-truths. Why study something that lacks credibility?
- ☐ I don't read, period! It's not just the Bible; I don't read anything.[1]

Can you identify with any of these sentiments? Make a check by any that sound familiar. If you're wrestling with one or more of these issues, we encourage you to share your struggle with your study leader.

10. What sources have been most influential in helping you understand prophecy to the degree that you do?

_____

_____

_____

_____

_____

_____

_____

_____

_____

Understanding the Word

Whatever reasons people give for not reading and studying the Bible, the fact remains that a huge blessing awaits those who *do* dig into God's Word. You are to be commended for embarking on this study. If you will make the effort to know and understand God's truth and if you will persevere in these lessons, you *will* find great blessing.

Consider the example of Ezra, a priest during Israel's time in exile. Notice his practice with regard to God's Word:

> *Ezra had determined to study and obey the law of the LORD and to teach those laws and regulations to the people of Israel.* (Ezra 7:10)

Ponder the response of the God-fearing Jews of Berea when the apostle Paul came and preached in their synagogue:

> *Now these were more noble-minded than those in Thessalonica, for they received the word with great eagerness, examining the Scriptures daily to see whether these things were so.* (Acts 17:11 NASB)

11. How did these different people from history approach God's Word? Do you see any common themes in these passages? What qualities in Ezra and the Bereans should we imitate?

_____

_____

_____

_____

_____

And then we have Paul's rousing counsel to Timothy, a leader in the early church:
> *Be diligent to present yourself approved to God as a workman who does not need to be ashamed, accurately handling the word of truth.* (2 Timothy 2:15 NASB)

12. What did Paul mean when, reminding Timothy of the need to handle God's Word with accuracy, he urged him to be a "diligent . . . workman"?

_____

_____

_____

_____

Second Timothy 3:16–17 says:

> *All Scripture is inspired by God and is useful to teach us what is true and to make us real-*
> *ize what is wrong in our lives. It straightens us out and teaches us to do what is right. It is*
> *God's way of preparing us in every way, fully equipped for every good thing God wants us*
> *to do.*

13. What does this passage tell us about the importance of studying the Bible? Based on the
Bible's purposes, in what ways do we benefit by studying what God's Word has to say
about the end times?

_____

_____

_____

_____

_____

_____

The Greek word Paul used in 2 Timothy 3:17 that is translated "fully equipped" was used in extrabiblical works to
describe a wagon outfitted for a long journey, or a rescue boat loaded with all necessary equipment. What a great picture! Speaking through Paul, God is telling us that if we make the effort to know and understand his Word (including
all that the Bible teaches about the end times), we will be equipped and ready for whatever we encounter along the
journey of life.

Finding the Connection

At the beginning of *Left Behind*, Rayford Steele is a worldly man. Like most people, he is busy
and distracted. He has no real interest in the Bible. He does not share his wife's hunger to
know God's truth, and so he is oblivious to what the Word of God says about most everything,
including the end times. The Bible, to Rayford, is nothing more than a quaint religious relic.
Because he sees the Scriptures as irrelevant to modern life, he chooses to remain ignorant as
to their content.

By contrast, Ezra, the Bereans, and Timothy made God's Word a priority. They followed in the footsteps of the psalmist who cried: "Truly, I love your commands more than gold, even the finest gold" (Psalm 119:127). They were eager to know what God had said. They diligently (and daily!) studied his Word. And—here's the crucial point—much of what they studied was prophetic material: that is, God's revelation about things to come. Bible teacher and scholar Charles Ryrie has written:

> It is said that one-fourth of the Bible was prophecy when it was written (of course many of those prophecies have already been fulfilled) and that one out of every five verses in Paul's writings concerns prophecy. . . .
>
> Furthermore, the Lord gave a promise to the disciples and to us concerning the teaching ministry of the Holy Spirit in this dispensation. He promised that the Spirit would "announce to you the things that are to come" (John 16:13 WILLIAMS). "Things that are to come" seems to be a specific area of truth within the broader promise that the Spirit "will guide you into all truth." In other words, special attention to prophecy is promised. Some understand those coming things not to refer to end-time events but to the revelation concerning the Christian church period (which was future when Christ spoke). Even if that interpretation is correct, "things that are to come" cannot exclude the events at the end of the church period, so . . . the Lord, then, expects us to understand prophecy.[2]

14. Before beginning this study, how much of the Bible would you have said has to do with the future? Now that you have a better idea of how much of Scripture contains prophetic material, how does that affect your interest in the study of biblical prophecy?

---

15. Why do you think God went to the trouble of giving the world a sneak peek at all that is to come?

---

16. Many people have argued that we really can't know for certain what the future holds—that the Bible is unclear, and that wise and godly scholars interpret all these "end-times" passages differently. How do you respond to this common viewpoint?

_____

_____

_____

_____

_____

17. Why do some of these same Christians have very strong opinions and convictions about other areas of theology—for instance, the doctrine of salvation or the doctrine of Christ? What is it about this whole subject of "last things" that makes so many believers hesitant to study and reluctant to arrive at firm convictions?

_____

_____

_____

_____

Making the Change

(*Left Behind*, pp. 209–10, 214)

Like so many people, Rayford Steele never gives God much thought until his whole world quite literally collapses. He waits until he is in serious trouble to take a hard look at the prophetic truths of Scripture.

In the novel he is given a videotape recorded by a Bible-believing pastor prior to the Rapture. (The pastor had "left behind" this tape, so that people "left behind" could understand the supernatural, prophetic events unfolding around them.) We enter the scene as the videotape begins, with the absent pastor speaking:

"THAT YOU ARE WATCHING indicates you have been left behind. You are no doubt stunned, shocked, afraid, and remorseful. I would like you to consider what I have to say here as instructions for life following Christ's rapture of his church. That is what has happened. Anyone you know or knew of who had placed his or her trust in Christ alone for salvation has been taken to heaven by Christ.

"Let me show you from the Bible exactly what has happened. You won't need this proof by now, because you will have experienced the most shocking event of history. But as this tape was made beforehand and I am confident that I will be gone, ask yourself, how did he know? Here's how, from 1 Corinthians 15:51–57."

The screen began to roll with the passage of Scripture. Rayford hit the pause button and ran to get Irene's Bible. It took him a while to find 1 Corinthians, and though it was slightly different in her translation, the meaning was the same.

The pastor said, "Let me read to you what the great missionary evangelist, the apostle Paul, wrote to the Christians at the church in the city of Corinth:

"Behold, I tell you a mystery: We shall not all sleep, but we shall all be changed— in a moment, in the twinkling of an eye, at the last trumpet. For the trumpet will sound, and the dead will be raised incorruptible, and we shall all be changed. For this corruptible must put on incorruption, and this mortal must put on immortality. So when this corruptible has put on incorruption, and this mortal has put on immortality, then shall be brought to pass the saying that is written: 'Death is swallowed up in victory. O Death, where is your sting? O Hades, where is your victory?' The sting of death is sin, and the strength of sin is the law. But thanks be to God, who gives us the victory through our Lord Jesus Christ."

Rayford was confused. He could follow some of that, but the rest was like gibberish to him. He let the tape roll. Pastor Billings continued, "Let me paraphrase some of that so you'll understand it clearly. When Paul says we shall not all sleep, he means that we shall not all die. And he's saying that this corruptible being must put on an incorruptible body which is to last for all eternity. When these things have happened, when the Christians who have already died and those that are still living receive their immortal bodies, the Rapture of the church will have taken place. . . .

"Bible prophecy is history written in advance. I urge you to find books on this subject or find people who may have been experts in this area but who for some reason did not receive Christ before and were left behind. Study so you'll know what is coming and how you can be prepared."

18. What are the advantages of knowing the prophecies of the Bible?

_____

_____

_____

_____

19. Is it enough just to know what the Bible predicts? What else must we do?

_____

_____

_____

_____

_____

20. If the Rapture happened today, how certain are you that you are ready to meet Christ in the air? Why?

_____

_____

_____

_____

_____

Pursuing the Truth

Philippians 2:14 says, "In everything you do, stay away from complaining and arguing." Acts 19:8 reports, "Then Paul went to the synagogue and preached boldly for the next three months, arguing persuasively about the Kingdom of God."

One passage forbids arguing, and yet the other says that the apostle Paul did little else but argue for three months straight. Is this a contradiction? Was Paul in sin? No. The word used by Paul in Philippians has a negative connotation. Taking the context into account, the passage is frowning on petty bickering and prideful disputes in which the goal is personal glory. The kind of "arguing" spoken of in Acts 19 is "reasoning and persuading." Paul's goal there was to make his case, to engage in thoughtful discussion and constructive dialogue.

When we begin any new Bible study, especially one in which Christians have various opinions, we need to ask God for a spirit of humility. We need to be open and teachable. We need to be willing to listen. It is possible to disagree without being disagreeable, to dialogue about ideas without destroying other people. When discussing these matters with those who do not yet know Christ, we need to defend the faith without becoming defensive, testy, or prickly.

21. What excites you as you think about embarking on this study? What intimidates you?

_____

_____

_____

_____

_____

_____

22. Someone has said that, among other things, biblical prophecy demonstrates:
    a. God's love and concern (that his creatures understand and prepare for what is to come);
    b. God's faithfulness (that what he says, he *will* do); and
    c. God's sovereignty (that the world—despite appearances—is *not* careening wildly out of control but moving toward its appointed end; God really *does* have the whole world—and all of human history—in his good, big hands).

    Does thinking about these traits of God make you less anxious about world events and the unknown future? In what way?

_____

_____

_____

_____

_____

"It is evident that God intended to draw aside the veil of the future and to give some indication of what His plans and purposes were for the human race and for the universe as a whole. . . .

"In the nature of Christian faith a solid hope for the future is essential. Christianity without a future would not be basic Christianity. In contrast, however, to the eschatology of heathen religions which often paints the future in a forbidding way, Christianity's hope is bright and clear and offers a Christian the basic fact that for a Christian the life to come is better than our present life. . . . In the Christian faith the future is painted as one of bliss and happiness in the presence of the Lord without the ills that are common to this life."[3]

John Walvoord

23. In what ways could this topic or this study be used by God in your life to prompt your friends, family, neighbors, colleagues, and classmates to consider the claims of Christ and the Bible?

_____

_____

_____

_____

_____

_____

24. What are your biggest questions about the end times? Write them in the space provided. Then over the course of this study, check once in a while to discover how many have been answered.

_____

_____

_____

_____

25. Consider signing the following commitment (particularly if you are beginning this study with a group).

Because I want to know what God has said about the future, I agree to the following:

☐ To diligently read, ponder, and study all Scripture passages in these lessons.
☐ To thoughtfully answer all questions.
☐ To earnestly ask God's Spirit to lead me into truth.
☐ To humbly open my heart and mind to what God is saying.
☐ To faithfully pray for others in this study.
☐ To boldly share what I am learning with others.

Signed on this date _____

by _____

Lesson in Review . . .

- Major blessings await those who study and apply God's Word.
- The Bible equips us for whatever life throws our way.
- A large percentage of the Bible was prophetic (i.e., future) at the time it was written.
- By following certain principles, we can grasp what the Bible says about the future.

LEFT

BIBLE STUDY GUIDE #1

BEHIND

The Rapture

Lesson 2
Instant Exit

1. What have you heard or what do you know about the Rapture?

2. Does the thought of the "end of the world" scare you? Why or why not?

3. You're driving in traffic and you notice a bumper sticker on the car in front of you that says, "WARNING: In case of the Rapture, this vehicle will be unmanned!" Do you:
   a. laugh
   b. shake your head over the gullibility of some people
   c. worry about the end of the world and your own soul
   d. keep talking on your cell phone/putting on makeup
   e. or other (if so, what?)

"I HEARD THE WORD 'RAPTURE' ISN'T EVEN IN THE BIBLE! IS THAT TRUE?"

"The English word comes from a Latin word, *rapio,* which means to seize or snatch in relation to an ecstasy of spirit or the actual removal from one place to another. In other words, it means to be carried away either in spirit or body. Thus the rapture of the church means the removal of the church from earth to heaven.

"But is this a biblical term? Yes. The Greek word from which we take this term rapture appears in 1 Thessalonians 4:17 and is translated 'caught up.' The Latin translation of this verse uses the word *rapturo,* from which we derive our English word rapture. So it is a biblical term that has come to us through the Latin translation of 1 Thessalonians 4:17."[1]

Charles Ryrie

Unfolding the Story

Left Behind, pp. 16–18

Book one of the Left Behind series begins with airline pilot Captain Rayford Steele and senior flight attendant Hattie Durham trying to come to grips with the sudden in-flight disappearance of more than a hundred passengers. The authors do a magnificent job of portraying the shock, confusion, and terror of those who will be left behind when Jesus Christ returns for his followers in the event commonly called "the Rapture."

"PEOPLE ARE MISSING," SHE MANAGED IN A WHISPER, burying her head in his chest. He took her shoulders and tried to push her back, but she fought to stay close. "What do you m——-?"

She was sobbing now, her body out of control. "A whole bunch of people, just gone!"

"Hattie, this is a big plane. They've wandered to the lavs or—"

She pulled his head down so she could speak directly into his ear. Despite her weeping, she was plainly fighting to make herself understood. "I've been everywhere. I'm telling you, dozens of people are missing."

"Hattie, it's still dark. We'll find—"

"I'm not crazy! See for yourself! All over the plane, people have disappeared."

"It's a joke. They're hiding, trying to—"

"Ray! Their shoes, their socks, their clothes, everything was left behind. These people are gone!"

28

. . . As he scanned the seats, he nearly panicked. He backed into a secluded spot behind the bulkhead and slapped himself hard on the cheek.

This was no joke, no trick, no dream. Something was terribly wrong, and there was no place to run. There would be enough confusion and terror without his losing control. Nothing had prepared him for this, and he would be the one everybody would look to. But for what? What was he supposed to do?

First one, then another cried out when they realized their seatmates were missing but that their clothes were still there. They cried, they screamed, they leaped from their seats. Hattie grabbed Rayford from behind and wrapped her hands so tight around his chest that he could hardly breathe. "Rayford, what is this?"

4. Put yourself in the shoes of one of these main characters from *Left Behind*. How do you think you would feel at this moment?

_____

_____

_____

_____

5. Imagine, at the moment of this earthshaking event, sitting in a football stadium filled with spectators, or driving in heavy traffic, or sitting in a big church service. What might it be like if people suddenly disappeared?

_____

_____

_____

6. With all the far-fetched things people do believe (alien abductions, Elvis sightings, etc.), why do you think so many scoff at the biblical notion of the Rapture?

_____

_____

_____

_____

Back to Reality

Even though many people are fascinated by the future and interested in the supernatural, there is another troubling reality at work. Most humans live for the moment and focus on the material things of this earth.

7. Why do you think people tend to be impulsive and unlikely to think about long-term consequences?

    _____

    _____

    _____

    _____

    _____

8. We all know we're going to die. We understand that there is "something" beyond this life, yet few people really grapple with those realities. Why the persistent ignoring of such an obvious issue?

    _____

    _____

    _____

    _____

    _____

9. What about you? By participating in this study you must have some interest in this topic. But do you tend to get so wrapped up in the "here and now" that you lose sight of eternal, spiritual realities, or have you developed a way to keep part of your attention always focused on God's purposes in history?

    _____

    _____

    _____

    _____

    _____

    _____

Understanding the Word

What a great and compassionate God we have! Rather than keeping his creatures in the dark about what is to come, he has graciously revealed the truth we need to be ready for the return of Christ.

The church at Thessalonica was established by the apostle Paul on his second missionary journey. Despite persecution, this young congregation stood strong and grew in the faith, having a tremendous impact, both near and far. Paul wrote them two letters of encouragement, intended to answer their questions and alleviate their concerns.

In the first letter, Paul addressed their confusion about the return of Christ and the fate of those believers who had already died.

> *And now, brothers and sisters, I want you to know what will happen to the Christians who have died so you will not be full of sorrow like people who have no hope. For since we believe that Jesus died and was raised to life again, we also believe that when Jesus comes, God will bring back with Jesus all the Christians who have died. I can tell you this directly from the Lord: We who are still living when the Lord returns will not rise to meet him ahead of those who are in their graves. For the Lord himself will come down from heaven with a commanding shout, with the call of the archangel, and with the trumpet call of God. First, all the Christians who have died will rise from their graves. Then, together with them, we who are still alive and remain on the earth will be caught up in the clouds to meet the Lord in the air and remain with him forever. So comfort and encourage each other with these words.* (1 Thessalonians 4:13–18)

10. How does Paul describe the Rapture of the church in this passage? What is the sequence of events?

_____

_____

_____

_____

_____

_____

_____

11. Why would these words and descriptions have been a comfort to Christians in the first century? In what way are they comforting to those living in the twenty-first century?

_____

_____

_____

_____

_____

_____

_____

12. As you read and contemplate this passage, do you feel encouraged, scared, or confused? How do you explain your response?

_____

_____

_____

_____

_____

_____

_____

13. In what ways do you understand the Rapture better based on the passage above and the plausible version of the event that you read in the novel? What questions do you still have about the Rapture?

_____

_____

_____

_____

_____

_____

_____

Finding the Connection

In *Left Behind*, Rayford and Hattie (along with millions of others!) were shocked and horrified to discover so many people suddenly "missing." Their fears turned to dread as they began to piece together the truth: that this cataclysmic event had been foretold in the Bible and that, rather than being left behind, they could have been among those who had been "caught up . . . in the clouds to meet the Lord in the air."

By contrast, in Thessalonica, a group of confused Christians were relieved and comforted to discover that they did not have to worry about fellow believers who had died, nor did they have to fret about what was to come. According to Paul, God is in control, and the future of the world is in his perfect, powerful hands.

The ancient group sought, questioned, and trusted, while the modern fictional group ignored God's truth and the warnings of his spokesmen. Why the difference? As we've noted, many people get so absorbed in the temporal aspects of life, they lose sight of the eternal realities.

Either the Bible is true or it is not. If it is (and there is no reason to conclude otherwise), then we are hurtling toward the end of human history. Hundreds of prophecies have already been fulfilled. The next great event on God's prophetic calendar is this event known as the Rapture.

Commenting on 1 Thessalonians 4, renowned prophecy scholar Dr. John Walvoord said:

> *Most significant in this passage is the fact that there are no preceding events, that is, there are no world-shaking events described as leading up to this event. As a matter of fact, the church down through the centuries could expect momentarily the Rapture of the church, which hope continues today. . . . The wonderful hope of the Rapture of the church is a source of constant encouragement to those who put their trust in Him and who are looking for His coming.*[2]

14. Is it hard for you to believe that Christ could come down from heaven for his saints at any moment? Explain.

_____

_____

_____

_____

_____

15. There are some who say that presenting biblical passages like this is nothing more than an attempt by Christians to scare people into following God. Do you agree? Why or why not?

_____

_____

_____

_____

_____

_____

16. How much of a role (if any) should fear play in making personal, theological, and spiritual decisions? Is there such a thing as "healthy" fear? What would that look like?

_____

_____

_____

_____

_____

17. If the Rapture were to occur today, do you have a settled sense that you would not be left behind? Why? On what do you base your belief?

_____

_____

_____

_____

_____

_____

Making the Change

Left Behind, pp. 195–96

Pastor and author Tony Evans makes this important point about studying the end times:

> *Bible prophecy is not designed to satisfy our curiosity about tomorrow or the next day, nor is it designed to fill our heads with information so we can get together and debate the details of God's plan. Gaining information has its place in the study of prophecy. It's important that we understand as fully as we can what God is saying to us. But at the heart of God's purpose for prophecy is changing our hearts and affecting the way we live our lives.*[3]

One of the main characters in the Left Behind books is a church staff member by the name of Bruce Barnes. Clearly this was an individual who knew a lot about God, but he did not know God personally. He understood the facts concerning the Rapture, but he was not personally ready. In his own words:

> **"I LOVED CHURCH.** It was my life, my culture. I thought I believed everything there was to believe in the Bible. . . . I knew other verses. . . . I even went to Bible college. . . . I had a real racket going, and I bought into it. Down deep, way down deep, I knew better. I knew it was too good to be true. I knew that true Christians were known by what their lives produced and that I was producing nothing."

18. Bruce basically admitted to being a hypocrite. He believed certain Bible facts on an intellectual level, but he never was transformed at the heart level. His admission reminds us that one of the more frequent criticisms of the Christian faith is the hypocrisy of Christians. Is this a valid rap, do you think? Why or why not?

_____

_____

_____

_____

_____

_____

_____

19. If you think the church does have lots of "make-believers" mixed in with the true believers, how do you explain this? Why in the world would someone merely pretend to be a Christian?

_____

_____

_____

_____

_____

_____

20. How would you explain the difference between head knowledge and heart knowledge? Between true spirituality and mere religiosity?

_____

_____

_____

_____

_____

_____

Pursuing the Truth

In *Left Behind,* Bruce Barnes gives Rayford Steele a videotaped explanation of the biblical doctrine of the Rapture "left behind" by Pastor Billings (Note: we read an excerpt from this scene in lesson one). This electronic communiqué uses 1 Corinthians 15:51–58 in an attempt to give stunned unbelievers like Rayford insight into the events unfolding all about them. Here's the 1 Corinthians 15 passage again:

> But let me tell you a wonderful secret God has revealed to us. Not all of us will die, but we will all be transformed. It will happen in a moment, in the blinking of an eye, when the last trumpet is blown. For when the trumpet sounds, the Christians who have died will be raised with transformed bodies. And then we who are living will be transformed so that we will never die. For our perishable earthly bodies must be transformed into heavenly bodies that will never die. When this happens—when our perishable earthly bodies have been

transformed into heavenly bodies that will never die—then at last the Scriptures will come true: "Death is swallowed up in victory. O death, where is your victory? O death, where is your sting?" For sin is the sting that results in death, and the law gives sin its power. How we thank God, who gives us victory over sin and death through Jesus Christ our Lord! So, my dear brothers and sisters, be strong and steady, always enthusiastic about the Lord's work, for you know that nothing you do for the Lord is ever useless.

21. The word *transformed* is used five times in this short passage. Why is that significant? What is God's ultimate goal for us?

_____

_____

_____

_____

_____

_____

_____

22. How is the transformation that will take place at the Rapture different from the transformation that should be taking place in our lives every day (see Romans 12:1–2)?

_____

_____

_____

_____

_____

_____

IN THE TWINKLING OF AN EYE?

"The entire procedure will be instantaneous, not gradual. The Greek word for 'moment' [see 1 Corinthians 15:52] is the word from which the word *atom* comes. Because when the atom was discovered, it was thought to be indivisible, it was named 'atom.' Even though subsequently the atom was split, the word still means 'indivisible.' The rapture will occur in an indivisible instant of time, like the twinkling of the eye."[4]

Charles Ryrie

23. In light of the certainty and imminency (remember that word?) of the Rapture, how are we Christians supposed to live? (Hint: see 1 Corinthians 15:58.)

_____

_____

_____

_____

Read and consider memorizing the following short passage:

> *There are many rooms in my Father's home, and I am going to prepare a place for you. If this were not so, I would tell you plainly. When everything is ready, I will come and get you, so that you will always be with me where I am.* (John 14:2–3)

24. What is your gut-level reaction to this statement by Jesus Christ shortly before he was crucified, then died, and then rose again from the grave?

_____

_____

_____

_____

_____

Tony Evans asks some thoughtful questions in his book *The Best Is Yet to Be:*

> *If you knew Jesus was coming back at this time next year, would you be doing some things differently today? What if you knew He was coming back next month, next week, tomorrow—or even at the end of this day? Would you be in a real hurry to do some things differently? If so, you'd better start doing those things now, because there is nothing preventing Him from coming for His church today.*[6]

25. How do you respond to his questions?

_____

_____

_____

_____

RAPTURE FACTS AT A GLANCE

- The Lord himself will descend from his Father's house, where he is preparing a place for us (John 14:1–3 and 1 Thessalonians 4:16).
- He will come again to receive us to himself (John 14:1–3).
- He resurrects those who have fallen asleep in him (deceased believers whom we will not precede; 1 Thessalonians 4:14–15).
- The Lord shouts as he descends ("loud command," 1 Thessalonians 4:16 NIV). All this takes place in the "twinkling of an eye" (1 Corinthians 15:52).
- We will hear the voice of the archangel (perhaps to lead Israel during the seven years of Tribulation as he did in the Old Testament; 1 Thessalonians 4:16).
- We will also hear the trumpet call of God (1 Thessalonians 4:16), his last trumpet for the church. (Don't confuse this with the seventh trumpet of judgment on the world during the Tribulation in Revelation 11:15.)
- The dead in Christ will rise first. (The corruptible ashes of their dead bodies are made incorruptible and joined together with their spirit, which Jesus brings with him; 1 Thessalonians 4:16–17.)
- Then we who are alive and remain shall be changed (made incorruptible by having our bodies made "immortal"; 1 Corinthians 15:51, 53).
- Then we shall be caught up [raptured] together (1 Thessalonians 4:17).
- With them in the clouds (where dead and living believers will have a monumental reunion; 1 Thessalonians 4:17)
- To meet the Lord in the air (1 Thessalonians 4:17).
- To "receive you to myself." Jesus takes us to the Father's house "that where I am, there you may be also" (John 14:3).
- "And thus we shall always be with the Lord" (1 Thessalonians 4:17).
- The judgment seat of Christ (2 Corinthians 5:10). At the call of Christ for believers, he will judge all things. Christians will stand before the judgment seat of Christ (Romans 14:10; 2 Corinthians 5:10), described in detail in 1 Corinthians 3:11–15. This judgment prepares Christians for . . .
- The marriage supper of the Lamb. Just prior to his coming to earth in power and great glory, Christ will meet his bride, the church, and the marriage supper will take place. In the meantime, after the church is raptured, the world will suffer the unprecedented time of the wrath of God, which our Lord called the Great Tribulation (Matthew 24:21).[5]

Lesson in Review . . .

- The Bible predicts an event called the Rapture—the sudden "catching up" of believers to meet Christ in the air.
- This event is imminent—it could literally happen at any moment.
- When the Rapture occurs, those who have not already come to know Jesus through faith will be left behind.

LEFT

BIBLE STUDY GUIDE #1

BEHIND

The Rapture

Lesson 3
The Big Picture

1. What subjects in school did you really understand, and in what classes did you feel perpetually lost and clueless?

_____

_____

_____

_____

_____

2. What are some of your biggest unanswered questions about the end times?

_____

_____

_____

_____

_____

3. Name one truth or lesson you've come to better understand as a result of the first two lessons in this study guide.

_____

_____

_____

_____

Unfolding the Story

(Tribulation Force, pp. 26–30)

Tribulation Force, the second book in the Left Behind series, begins with a small group of new believers in Christ trying to grasp what the Bible says about the sequence of events in the end times.

In the opening pages we find Bruce Barnes, a longtime church staff member who was not a true believer until after the disappearance of millions of Christians in the event known as the Rapture. Bruce is speaking to his new brothers and sisters in Christ:

> "DON'T YOU SEE? WE KNOW NICOLAE CARPATHIA IS THE ANTICHRIST. . . . There's plenty of evidence that Carpathia fits the prophetic descriptions. . . . The news that really got me today was the announcement that the next major order of business for Carpathia is what he calls 'an understanding' between the global community and Israel. . . ."
>
> Chloe looked up. "And that actually signals the beginning of the seven-year period of tribulation."
>
> "Exactly." Bruce looked at the group. "If that announcement says anything about a promise from Carpathia that Israel will be protected over the next seven years, it officially ushers in the Tribulation."
>
> Buck was taking notes. "So the disappearances, the Rapture, didn't start the seven-year period?"
>
> "No," Bruce said. "Part of me hoped that something would delay the treaty with Israel. Nothing in Scripture says it has to happen right away. But once it does, the clock starts ticking."
>
> "But it starts ticking toward Christ setting up his kingdom on earth, right?" Buck asked. Rayford was impressed that Buck had learned so much so quickly.
>
> Bruce nodded. "That's right. And that's the reason for this meeting. I need to tell you all something. I am going to have a two-hour meeting, right here in this office, every weeknight from eight to ten. Just for us. . . . I can't force you to come, but I urge you. Anytime you're in town, be here. In our studies, we're going to outline what God has revealed in the Scriptures. Some of it you've already heard me talk about. But if the treaty with Israel comes within the next few days, we have no time to waste. We need to be starting new churches, new cell groups of believers. I want to go to Israel and hear the two witnesses at the Wailing Wall. The Bible talks about 144,000

Jews springing up and traveling throughout the world. There is to be a great soul harvest, maybe a billion or more people, coming to Christ."

"That sounds fantastic," Chloe said. "We should be thrilled."

"I am thrilled," Bruce said. "But there will be little time to rejoice or rest. Remember the seven Seal Judgments Revelation talks about?" She nodded. "Those will begin immediately, if I'm right. There will be an eighteen-month period of peace, but in the three months following that, the rest of the Seal Judgments will fall on the earth. One-fourth of the world's population will be wiped out."

4. Some might read that passage and think, "A two-hour Bible study every night! Isn't that a bit excessive?" Why did the Tribulation Force agree to do this?

    _____

    _____

    _____

    _____

5. Bruce and the others seemed excited about certain looming events and overwhelmed by others. Why?

    _____

    _____

    _____

    _____

Back to Reality

When we close the exciting novels and return to real life, the possibilities portrayed in the stories ought to open our eyes to our world in a fresh way. At the very least, they ought to drive us to an attitude of humble prayer before God, who remains in control of the events of history.

6. If in Scripture God *has* revealed huge details about what is to come, why do you think so many people (including many Christians) remain so clueless?

    _____

    _____

_____

_____

7. Say a team of renowned historians told you with absolute certainty that a pirate's chest filled with treasure lay buried somewhere on your property and legally belonged to you. How would you respond?

_____

_____

_____

_____

8. Why do you think so many Christians are unwilling to dig into the Word of God for the "treasure" of knowing more about what lies ahead?

_____

_____

_____

_____

Understanding the Word

So far in this study guide we've looked at the facts of biblical prophecy and the importance of understanding what is revealed about the "last days" (lesson one). Then we focused our attention on the imminent disappearance of millions of Christians from the earth, the Rapture (lesson two). It is that "blessed hope" of Christians—meeting Christ in the air and going with him to heaven—that will set the stage for the rapid-fire sequence of last-days events foretold in the Bible. Now we want to turn our attention to the big picture as illustrated by the novel and taught in Scripture.

9. Is Bruce's explanation above just his own fanciful thinking, or is the outline he proposed something God has revealed in the pages of the Bible?

_____

_____

_____

We believe a careful study of the "whole counsel" of God's Word suggests the following sequence of events during the earth's "last days":

The Great Apostasy

The Rapture

The Rise of the Antichrist

The Tribulation

The Great Tribulation

The "Glorious Appearing"

The Millennium

The Last Rebellion

The Great White Throne Judgment

The Eternal State

Let's look briefly at each of those key events and where they are found in God's Word. (We'll skip the Rapture since we already spent a whole session on the subject.)

The Great Apostasy

Now the Holy Spirit tells us clearly that in the last times some will turn away from what we believe; they will follow lying spirits and teachings that come from demons. These teachers are hypocrites and liars. They pretend to be religious, but their consciences are dead. They will say it is wrong to be married and wrong to eat certain foods. But God created those foods to be eaten with thanksgiving by people who know and believe the truth. Since everything God created is good, we should not reject any of it. We may receive it gladly, with thankful hearts (1 Timothy 4:1–4).

10. *Apostasy* means to rebel or depart from the truth. In some parts of the world we see millions embracing Christ, and in other places we see wide-scale rejection of the things of God. How do you explain this? (For more insight, see 2 Thessalonians 2:1–3; 2 Timothy 3:1–5; 4:1–4.)

_____

_____

_____

_____

_____

"False teachers rarely exist in a spiritual vacuum. They start appearing because people want to hear and act on their flesh-stroking doctrines. In many ways, spirituality is as much a commodity as is electronics or beef and is subject to similar laws of supply and demand. In this passage (1 Timothy 4:1–4) Paul says carnal people 'gather around them a great number of teachers to say what their itching ears want to hear.' In other words, the people demand to hear ungodly fables, and soon false teachers start appearing to supply the demand—like flies to a garbage dump."[1]

Tim LaHaye and Jerry Jenkins

The Rapture (see lesson one)

The Rise of the Antichrist

> *Don't be fooled by what they say. For that day will not come until there is a great rebellion against God and the man of lawlessness is revealed—the one who brings destruction. He will exalt himself and defy every god there is and tear down every object of adoration and worship. He will position himself in the temple of God, claiming that he himself is God. Don't you remember that I told you this when I was with you? And you know what is holding him back, for he can be revealed only when his time comes. For this lawlessness is already at work secretly, and it will remain secret until the one who is holding it back steps out of the way. Then the man of lawlessness will be revealed, whom the Lord Jesus will consume with the breath of his mouth and destroy by the splendor of his coming. This evil man will come to do the work of Satan with counterfeit power and signs and miracles. He will use every kind of wicked deception to fool those who are on their way to destruc- tion because they refuse to believe the truth that would save them. (2 Thessalonians 2:3–10)*

11. What does this passage tell you about "the man of lawlessness" (i.e., the Antichrist)? (For more insight, see Daniel 7:8–26; 11:36–45; and Revelation 13:3–8.)

_____

_____

_____

_____

_____

"The Antichrist will arrive on the world scene with an olive branch, but concealed beneath the branch is a sword. His conquest of other nations will soon overshadow his covenant with Israel. In Daniel 11 the prophet tore off the façade to reveal the underlying motives of the Antichrist. His actions will stem from his pride and his thirst for power. Though he might appear initially as a man of humility, his ultimate goal in all his actions will be to exalt himself. 'He will show no regard for the gods of his fathers or for the one desired by women [a deity worshiped by women], nor will he regard any god, but will exalt himself above them all' (11.37). The Antichrist will be the ultimate product of the 'Me' generation."[2]

Charles H. Dyer

The Tribulation (including the Great Tribulation)

"The time will come when you will see what Daniel the prophet spoke about: the sacrilegious object that causes desecration standing in the holy place"—reader, pay attention! "Then those in Judea must flee to the hills. A person outside the house must not go inside to pack. A person in the field must not return even to get a coat. How terrible it will be for pregnant women and for mothers nursing their babies in those days. And pray that your flight will not be in winter or on the Sabbath. For that will be a time of greater horror than anything the world has ever seen or will ever see again. In fact, unless that time of calamity is shortened, the entire human race will be destroyed. But it will be shortened for the sake of God's chosen ones." (Matthew 24:15–22)

12. In this teaching, part of what is called the Olivet Discourse, how did Jesus describe the coming seven-year period (see Daniel 9:24–27) commonly known as the Tribulation?

_____

_____

_____

13. Since Jesus' opening remarks about the destruction of the temple were fulfilled down to the last detail by the invading Romans in A.D. 70, what can we conclude about the accuracy of the other prophecies found in his remarks in Matthew 24 and 25? (For further study and more details, see Revelation 6, 8, 9, 15, 16.)

_____

_____

No other event in the Bible, except perhaps the Second Coming itself, is mentioned more frequently than the Tribulation. It is so important that we cannot cover it all, even in the twelve books of the Left Behind series. There is no end to the astonishing events from this awful period. . . . No wonder Jesus said the Tribulation was unique from anything that has ever happened or would happen again![3]

Tim LaHaye and Jerry Jenkins

The "Glorious Appearing"

For as the lightning lights up the entire sky, so it will be when the Son of Man comes. . . . Immediately after those horrible days end, the sun will be darkened, the moon will not give light, the stars will fall from the sky, and the powers of heaven will be shaken. And then at last, the sign of the coming of the Son of Man will appear in the heavens, and there will be deep mourning among all the nations of the earth. And they will see the Son of Man arrive on the clouds of heaven with power and great glory. And he will send forth his angels with the sound of a mighty trumpet blast, and they will gather together his chosen ones from the farthest ends of the earth and heaven. (Matthew 24:27, 29–31)

14. Think about Christ's first coming (see Matthew 1 and Luke 2). How does that compare with the way the Bible passage above describes his second coming? (For further study and more details, see Zechariah 14:1–11 and Revelation 19:11–16.)

"Christ returns the second time to fulfill his God-given role as King, a role appointed to him by the Father at his ascension (Psalm 2:6–7; 110:1). He was introduced in that role by his appointed forerunner, John (Matthew 3:2), and claimed that right himself (Matthew 4:17). When the multitudes witnessed a spectacular miracle, they acknowledged that Christ was the Messiah, the son of David (Matthew 12:23). At the Second Advent, he appears as 'KING OF KINGS AND LORD OF LORDS' (Revelation 19:16). His glory will be revealed throughout the thousand years of his reign here on earth (Revelation 20:2–3) as David's 'son' in David's kingdom, as covenanted by God with Israel (2 Samuel 7:16; Psalm 89:3–4).

"The believer anticipates the glory that will be revealed at His coming (see Titus 2:13), for we will share His glory. This hope (settled assurance) is a source of blessing while we await the revelation of His glory: His glory as a Judge, His glory as a Deliverer, and His glory as King."[4]

J. Dwight Pentecost

The Millennium (see Revelation 20:1–6)

15. How will the world be different when the enemies of God have been vanquished and the all-powerful Lord Jesus Christ is ruling? (For further details about the future earthly reign of Christ, see Isaiah 2, 11, 19, and 35.)

_____

_____

The Last Rebellion (see Revelation 20:7–10)

The Great White Throne Judgment (see Revelation 20:11–15)
(For further details read Romans 2:5–6.)

"The Bible says, 'There is no condemnation in Christ,' and yet I heard that Christians will have to stand before God and be judged! What's the truth?"
"The truth is that Christians *will* give an account of our lives to Christ. This will occur in heaven, probably after the Rapture and before the Second Coming/Glorious Appearing, at the judgment seat of Christ (see 2 Corinthians 5:10). The Greek word translated 'judgment seat' in this verse is *bema* (pronounced bay-mah), which was the name of the raised platform in the Isthmian Games (a kind of ancient 'Olympics' competition in Corinth, Greece), where prizes were given to the winning athletes. In short, our lives and motivations *will* be evaluated and faithful service to Christ will be rewarded (see 1 Corinthians 3:10–13).

"Remember, no believer in Christ will stand before God at the great white throne. That terrible spot is reserved for those who have rejected Christ as Savior, who have decided to crown themselves king, and who have refused to accept Jesus Christ as their true Lord.

"Do not make that terrible mistake! Instead, place your faith in the Lord Jesus and ask him to forgive your sins; then you will be ready 'to stand before the Son of Man' (Luke 21:36) at the judgment seat of Christ."[5]

Tim LaHaye and Jerry Jenkins

The Eternal State (see Revelation 21–22)

16. What most excites you about eternity?

_____

_____

17. What most confuses or concerns you?

_____

_____

Finding the Connection

There are plenty of other end-times events that warrant our study and attention. The nature of this lesson does not permit a detailed discussion of the rebuilding of the temple in Jerusalem, the rise and fall of Babylon, the false prophet, the two witnesses, or the 144,000 Jewish witnesses. We will look at those events and/or end-times characters in other study guides.

18. Studies have shown that repeated exposure to violent and graphic images (even simulated ones) has a way of numbing people to the real thing. The lines between fantasy and reality become blurred, so that people barely yawn when they see horrific scenes in real life. Do you think some people have seen so many special effects-laden movies and TV shows that they have a hard time believing the amazing end-times events described in the Bible will actually happen? Explain.

_____

_____

_____

19. Imagine a friend sees you reading your Bible—say, the book of Revelation—or one of the Left Behind books. The friend then asks, "What does the Bible say about the end of the world?" What answer would you give?

_____

_____

_____

"As soon as the church is raptured, God will again begin to visibly intervene in the affairs of mankind. Russia and her allies will go down to destroy the nation of Israel, but will themselves be destroyed supernaturally by God (Ezekiel 38–39). No one knows for sure whether that precedes or follows the Rapture; a case can be made either way. One thing is apparent: Russia's attack and the Rapture are the number one and two end-time events. They are followed by the rise of Antichrist, the day of God's wrath, the two witnesses, the 144,000 Jewish evangelists, and many other acts of divine intervention during the Tribulation. There will be so many signs that atheism will not be widespread during that period; amazingly, it will be supplanted by open and blatant rebellion against God.

"The Tribulation will be followed by the majestic intervention of God in the glorious return of Christ to the earth to set up his thousand-year kingdom, followed by heaven or eternity. . . . The good news is that this world will not end in chaos as the secularists predict. The Bible says Christ will come to solve the world's problems by introducing the greatest period in world history, the millennial kingdom of Jesus Christ. And while we are not certain it will occur in our lifetime, we have more reason to believe it might than any generation in the history of the church."[6]

Tim LaHaye & Jerry Jenkins

Making the Change

(*Left Behind*, p. 468)

At the very end of *Left Behind*, we find this passage:

> THEY MOVED THROUGH THE TERMINAL toward the parking garage, striding four
> abreast, arms around each other's shoulders, knit with a common purpose. Rayford
> Steele, Chloe Steele, Buck Williams, and Bruce Barnes faced the gravest dangers any-
> one could face, and they knew their mission.
>
> The task of the Tribulation Force was clear and their goal nothing less than to
> stand and fight the enemies of God during the seven most chaotic years the planet
> would ever see.

Their brave resolve reminds us of the old truth: knowing what to do must be translated into doing what we know. In other words, the purpose of all Bible knowledge is life change! After we comprehend the truth, it's time to live it out. Let's think through some of the implications of this lesson.

20. If a Christian took biblical prophecy to heart and really believed that the return of Christ is imminent, how would it change his or her daily routine? Give some specific examples.

_____

_____

_____

21. What kind of response or reaction might greet a Christian who suddenly became convinced that time is running short and who adjusted his or her beliefs and behavior accordingly?

_____

_____

_____

22. In a heated discussion with some of Israel's religious leaders, Jesus made this statement: *"The Devil . . . was a murderer from the beginning and has always hated the truth. There is no truth in him. When he lies, it is consistent with his character; for he is a liar and the father of lies"* (John 8:44). Knowing the aggressive, deceptive nature of Satan, how should we alter our lives today? How can we resist getting swept up in the delusions that capture so many?

_____

_____

_____

Pursuing the Truth

Consider the following Bible passages:

You will keep in perfect peace all who trust in you, whose thoughts are fixed on you! (Isaiah 26:3)

And now, dear friends, let me say one more thing as I close this letter. Fix your thoughts on what is true and honorable and right. Think about things that are pure and lovely and admirable. Think about things that are excellent and worthy of praise. (Philippians 4:8)

Let heaven fill your thoughts. Do not think only about things down here on earth. (Colossians 3:2)

23. What do these verses say about our "mind-set"? What is the effect of this kind of God-honoring thinking in uncertain times?

_____
_____
_____
_____

Tim LaHaye and Jerry Jenkins write:

The second coming of Jesus Christ, and the many lesser events leading up to it and following it, is what prophecy is primarily about. It is doubtless the greatest story of the future to be found anywhere. No religion, no culture, and no literature offers such a sublime concept of future events that lead into an even better eternity. Once understood, these thrilling events prove so exciting and inspiring that many have turned from their sins to find Christ as their Lord and Savior—a good reason for all Christians to know about them, particularly as we see so many of these events fulfilled in our lifetime. [7]

24. Do *you* believe you are part of the generation that will see these events unfold? Why or why not?

_____
_____
_____

25. What wise and practical counsel does the following passage give for your life today?

Therefore be patient, brethren, until the coming of the Lord. The farmer waits for the precious produce of the soil, being patient about it, until it gets the early and late rains. You too be patient; strengthen your hearts, for the coming of the Lord is near. Do not complain, brethren, against one another, so that you yourselves may not be judged; behold, the Judge is standing right at the door. (James 5:7–9 NASB)

_____
_____

"Biblical prophecy . . . involves a lot of details, and they're important. Libraries full of books have been written to discuss and examine the details of God's prophetic drama. . . . But before we put God's prophetic Word under the microscope, we need to put it up on the big screen, so to speak, and see the full picture. We need to get the program in proper focus, and to do that we need to understand the key to Bible prophecy.

"A key is important because it gives you access. A key that will unlock Bible prophecy, helping you see the individual details in their proper relationship and keep them in proper perspective, is hanging at the 'door' of Revelation 19:10. After another awe-inspiring revelation by an angel, John was about to fall at the angel's feet in worship. But the angel told John, 'Do not do that; I am a fellow servant of yours and your brethren who hold the testimony of Jesus; worship God. For the testimony of Jesus is the spirit of prophecy.'

"That's a profoundly important statement. It tells us that the key that unlocks the door to prophecy is not a thing or an idea, but a person. Jesus Christ is the key to God's prophetic revelation. . . . God did not simply string together a series of prophetic events that happen one after another. There's a point, a definite climax to God's plan. Prophecy, like history, is taking us somewhere. And that destination is Jesus Christ. So if we study the details and yet miss Christ, we have missed the point of prophecy."[8]

Tony Evans

Lesson in Review . . .

- God has not left the human race in the dark about what is to come. The Bible is filled with clues about the future!
- Through careful study, we can fit the pieces of God's prophetic puzzle together.
- Knowing what is to come means we alter our lives accordingly—living rightly and speaking boldly to others.

The Rapture

Lesson 4
One Coming—Two Phases

In his excellent book *The Best Is Yet to Come,* pastor Tony Evans writes:

> *Early Edition was a popular television program in the 1990s that featured a young man who regularly received the next day's newspaper a day ahead of time. Because he always knew the future, this man's task in each episode was to save people from a tragedy or problem he had read about in tomorrow's paper. So if he knew a building was going to burn, he tried to keep people from entering it. Or if someone was going to be hurt by an act of violence or in an accident, he tried to prevent the encounter from taking place.*
>
> *We who hold God's prophetic word in our hands also have an "early edition" of future events. We have God's plan for all eternity, the unfolding of his eternal drama that will culminate for believers in the glories of heaven.*[1]

1. With such heavy emphasis on the end times in the Bible, and with so much riding on a proper understanding of future events, why do you think this subject is so rarely discussed in many modern churches?

   _____

   _____

   _____

2. In what ways do you think the emphasis (or lack of) on the imminent return of Christ affects the quality of spiritual living that you see people experiencing in your local church?

   _____

   _____

   _____

Unfolding the Story

(*Left Behind,* pp. 211–13, 308–09)

Left Behind features a wise and compassionate character named Vernon Billings, pastor of New Hope Community Church. We don't actually ever meet Rev. Billings in person. By the time he appears on the pages of the story, he's been caught up into heaven with all the other Christians on earth. We see and hear this godly man only via a videotape that he has lovingly prepared to help those left behind.

Scared and confused, Rayford Steele watches this Rapture video to try to understand how the shocking events all around him are actually foretold in the Bible. This is what Rayford hears:

> "PAUL'S PROPHETIC LETTER TO THE CORINTHIANS said this would occur in the twinkling of an eye. You may well have seen a loved one standing before you, and suddenly they were gone. I don't envy you that shock.
>
> "The Bible says that men's hearts will fail them for fear. That means to me that there will be heart attacks due to shock, people will commit suicide in their despair, and you know better than I the chaos that will result from Christians disappearing from various modes of transportation, with a loss of firefighters and police officers and emergency workers of all sorts.
>
> "Depending on when you're viewing this tape, you may have already found that martial law is in effect in many places, emergency measures trying to keep evil elements from looting and fighting over the spoils of what is left. Governments will tumble and there will be international disorder.
>
> "You may wonder why this has happened. Some believe this is the judgment of God on an ungodly world. Actually, that is to come later. Strange as this may sound to you, this is God's final effort to get the attention of every person who has ignored or rejected him. He is allowing now a vast period of trial and tribulation to come to you who remain. He has removed his church from a corrupt world that seeks its own way, its own pleasures, its own ends.
>
> "I believe God's purpose in this is to allow those who remain to take stock of themselves and leave their frantic search for pleasure and self-fulfillment, and turn to the Bible for truth and to Christ for salvation.
>
> "Let me encourage you that your loved ones, your children and infants, your friends, and your acquaintances have not been snatched away by some evil force or

some invasion from outer space. That will likely be a common explanation. What sounded ludicrous to you before might sound logical now, but it is not.

"Also, Scripture indicates that there will be a great lie, announced with the help of the media and perpetrated by a self-styled world leader. Jesus himself prophesied about such a person. He said, 'I have come in my father's name, and you do not receive me; if another comes in his own name, him you will receive.'

"I believe the Bible teaches that the Rapture of the church ushers in a seven-year period of trial and tribulation, during which terrible things will happen. If you have not received Christ as your Savior, your soul is in jeopardy. And because of the cataclysmic events that will take place during this period, your very life is in danger. If you turn to Christ, you may still have to die as a martyr."

Later, Bruce Barnes, a longtime pastoral associate of Rev. Billings, but a true believer in Jesus only since the Rapture, gathers some other new converts and spiritual seekers in an attempt to help them more fully grasp the scriptural teaching about the end times. Here's what he tells them:

"AS YOU KNOW, I'VE BEEN STUDYING Revelation and several commentaries about end-times events. Well, today in the pastor's files I ran across one of his sermons on the subject. I've been reading the Bible and the books on the subject, and here's what I found."

Bruce pulled up the first blank sheet on a flip chart and showed a time line he had drawn. "I'll take the time to carefully teach you this over the next several weeks, but it looks to me, and to many of the experts who came before us, that this period of history we're in right now will last for seven years. . . . That last half of the seven years is called the Great Tribulation, and if we're alive at the end of it, we will be rewarded by seeing the Glorious Appearing of Christ.". . .

"If we die, we will be in heaven with Christ and our loved ones. But we may suffer horrible deaths. If we somehow make it through the seven terrible years, especially the last half, the Glorious Appearing will be all that more glorious. Christ will come back to set up his thousand-year reign on earth."

3. How do you imagine Rayford Steele feels as he watched this videotape? What regrets might he have? How does a person in such a situation not give in to utter despair?

_____
_____
_____

4. Pastor Billings and Bruce Barnes both seem to be describing the coming of Christ, and yet their explanations are *not* identical. How do you explain this?

_____
_____
_____
_____
_____

Back to Reality

God used cataclysmic, real-world events and a "left behind" video to communicate his truth to the characters in the Left Behind books.

5. What are some of the ways God typically tries to get the attention of people today? When in your life has God given you a "wake-up" call? What happened?

_____
_____
_____
_____
_____

6. Do you have anyone in your life like a Pastor Billings? Who is it? Describe the impact this person is having or has had on you personally.

_____
_____
_____
_____
_____

7. Even though he was a lifelong churchgoer, a Bible college graduate, and even a church staff member, Bruce Barnes was *not* a true Christian—at least, not until after the Rapture. How is it possible to be surrounded by the trappings of Christianity and yet still not possess a real, personal faith?

    _____

    _____

    _____

    _____

    _____

    _____

    _____

Understanding the Word

It's not just fictional characters like Rayford Steele and Hattie Durham who are confused about end-times events. Lots of real people are confused too (perhaps even you). One common area of misunderstanding has to do with the return of Christ. In some passages, the primary emphasis seems to be on Christians going up to heaven, whereas in other texts, the main point seems to be that Christ is coming down (or back) to earth.

A careful look at some of the key Scriptures can help us understand an important distinction. Look first at one of the most important passages in the New Testament regarding the Rapture:

> And now, brothers and sisters, I want you to know what will happen to the Christians who have died so you will not be full of sorrow like people who have no hope. For since we believe that Jesus died and was raised to life again, we also believe that when Jesus comes, God will bring back with Jesus all the Christians who have died.
>
> I can tell you this directly from the Lord: We who are still living when the Lord returns will not rise to meet him ahead of those who are in their graves. For the Lord himself will come down from heaven with a commanding shout, with the call of the archangel, and with the trumpet call of God. First, all the Christians who have died will rise from their graves. Then, together with them, we who are still alive and remain on the earth will be caught up in the clouds to meet the Lord in the air and remain with him forever. So comfort and encourage each other with these words. (1 Thessalonians 4:13–18)

8. How is this future event described? What specific phrases are used? Make a short list of the primary "ingredients" or aspects of this event.

_____

_____

_____

_____

_____

_____

Now consider this prophetic passage from the apostle John's Revelation of Jesus Christ:

Then I saw heaven opened, and a white horse was standing there. And the one sitting on the horse was named Faithful and True. For he judges fairly and then goes to war. His eyes were bright like flames of fire, and on his head were many crowns. A name was written on him, and only he knew what it meant. He was clothed with a robe dipped in blood, and his title was the Word of God. The armies of heaven, dressed in pure white linen, followed him on white horses. From his mouth came a sharp sword, and with it he struck down the nations. He ruled them with an iron rod, and he trod the winepress of the fierce wrath of almighty God. On his robe and thigh was written this title: King of kings and Lord of lords.

Then I saw an angel standing in the sun, shouting to the vultures flying high in the sky: "Come! Gather together for the great banquet God has prepared. Come and eat the flesh of kings, captains, and strong warriors; of horses and their riders; and of all humanity, both free and slave, small and great."

Then I saw the beast gathering the kings of the earth and their armies in order to fight against the one sitting on the horse and his army. And the beast was captured, and with him the false prophet who did mighty miracles on behalf of the beast—miracles that deceived all who had accepted the mark of the beast and who worshiped his statue. Both the beast and his false prophet were thrown alive into the lake of fire that burns with sulfur. Their entire army was killed by the sharp sword that came out of the mouth of the one riding the white horse. And all the vultures of the sky gorged themselves on the dead bodies.

Then I saw an angel come down from heaven with the key to the bottomless pit and a heavy chain in his hand. He seized the dragon—that old serpent, the Devil, Satan—and bound him in chains for a thousand years. (Revelation 19:11–20:2)

9. How is *this* future event described?

_____

_____

_____

_____

_____

10. What similarities do you see between the two passages? What differences?

_____

_____

_____

_____

_____

11. What clues do you find in your investigation to suggest these passages are speaking of two different events?

_____

_____

_____

_____

_____

> "When the more than three hundred Bible references to the Second Coming are carefully examined, it becomes clear that there are two phases to his return. There are far too many conflicting activities connected with his return to be merged into a single coming. . . . Most scholars who take the Bible literally wherever possible believe he is talking about one 'coming' in two stages. First, he will come suddenly in the air to rapture his church and take believers to his Father's house, in fulfillment of his promise in John 14:1–3. . . . Second, he will finish his second coming by returning to the earth gloriously and publicly in great power to set up his kingdom. . . . Dr. David L. Cooper often compares the Second Coming to a two-act play separated by a seven-year intermission (the Tribulation). The apostle Paul distinguished these two events in Titus 2:13 by designating them 'the blessed hope and glorious appearing.' "[2]
>
> Tim LaHaye and Jerry Jenkins

Bible References to the Rapture	Bible References to the Second Coming
PRIMARY	*PRIMARY*
John 14:1–3	Matthew 24:15–31
1 Corinthians 15:51–53	Revelation 19:11–20:6
1 Thessalonians 4:13–18	
SECONDARY	*SECONDARY*
Romans 8:19	Daniel 2:44–45; 7:9–14; 12:1–3
1 Corinthians 16:22	Zechariah 12:10; 14:1–15
Philippians 3:20–21; 4:5	Matthew 13:41; 26:64
Colossians 3:4	Mark 13:14–27; 14:62
1 Thessalonians 1:10; 2:19; 5:9, 23	Luke 21:25–28
2 Thessalonians 2:1	Acts 1:9–11; 3:19–21
1 Timothy 6:14	1 Thessalonians 3:13
2 Timothy 4:1, 8	2 Thessalonians 1:6–10; 2:8
Titus 2:13	1 Peter 4:12–13
Hebrews 9:28	2 Peter 3:1–14
James 5:7–9	Jude 1:14–15
1 Peter 1:7, 13; 5:4	Revelation 1:7; 22:7, 12, 20
1 John 2:28–3:2	
Jude 1:21	
Revelation 2:25; 3:10	

Finding the Connection

Some people argue, "Why all the fuss over all these details of Scripture? Does it *really* matter if Christ's coming is in one phase, or two, or fifteen stages? Isn't the important thing that we believe he is coming back, period? Why haggle over the meaning of all these different passages?"

12. How would you respond to these comments and questions?

_____

_____

_____

_____

_____

_____

"Do you ever wonder sometimes whether the Bible is just a giant riddle? God intended it as a revelation. Second Timothy 3:16 says, 'All Scripture is *profitable*' (italics added). That is, it has purpose, it has meaning. God is not playing a game of hide-and-seek with you. He doesn't invite you into his Word only to puzzle and confound you. He's far more interested that you understand it than you are.

"But the question is, what do we mean by 'meaning'? Let me give you an illustration. I happen to be partially color-blind, so I can't easily distinguish between greens and blues. Suppose you showed me a sweater and said, 'Prof, I just love this blue sweater.' We would both be looking at the same sweater, but the color you see would not be the same as the color I see.

"That happens all the time in biblical interpretation. Two people will look at the same verse and come up with two completely different interpretations. In fact, they may be opposing interpretations. Can they both be correct? Not if the laws of logic apply to Scripture. But unfortunately, many people today have decided that the laws of logic do not apply to Scripture. To them, it doesn't really matter whether you see the text as blue and I see it as green. In fact, it doesn't really matter what color the text actually is. For them, the meaning of the text is not in the text, it's in their response to the text. And everyone is free to have his or her own response. Meaning becomes purely subjective.

"Now there are good reasons Christians may disagree on the interpretation of a passage. . . . But if we're to have any hope of interpreting God's Word accurately, we've got to start with a fundamental premise: 'Meaning' is not our subjective thoughts read into the text but God's objective truth read out of the text. As someone has well said, the task of Bible study is to 'think God's thoughts after Him.' He has a mind, and He has revealed it in His Word."[3]

Howard Hendricks

13. Does the excerpt by Howard Hendricks above alter in any way how you look at the details of God's Word? If so, how?

_____

_____

14. Why can't we interpret the passages about the return of Christ in "any old way"?

_____

_____

_____

15. Look at the following chart. Compare its data to the observations you made in questions 10 and 11. Can you think of any other distinguishing features between the "blessed hope" and the "Glorious Appearing"?

_____

_____

_____

_____

Some of the Primary Differences Between the Rapture (Blessed Hope)
and the Second Coming (Glorious Appearing)

The Rapture	The Second Coming
Secret (only his own will see him)	Public (every eye will see him)
Affects a special group, the church	Affects the whole world
To gather living and dead Christians	To judge those who have rejected Christ
Happens in the air	Occurs on the earth
Rapture (i.e., snatching away) of Christians	No rapture
No judgment on earth	Judgment on earth
Could happen at any moment	Follows the seven-year Tribulation period
No warning signs given	Many signs given
Christians taken immediately to their heavenly Father's house	Resurrected saints remain on earth for the millennial kingdom
No mention of Satan	Satan bound for 1,000 years
Sets the stage for the seven-year Tribulation to begin	Inaugurates the 1,000 year millennial rule of Christ

Making the Change

What do people typically do when . . .

something *wonderful* happens to them?

something *terrible* happens to them?

something *sobering and life changing* happens to them?

The answer? They tell other people about it. That's just human nature. We can't keep good stuff, momentous news, or difficulties to ourselves.

16. If that's true, then what do you need to do with all that you're learning about the return of Christ? In your heart of hearts, do you believe it? Do you see all this Rapture talk and prophecy study as "religious wishful thinking," or as the certain time line for earth's not-so-distant future?

_____

_____

_____

_____

_____

_____

As Rayford Steele becomes more convinced of the Bible's end-times truth, he feels more of a conviction to tell others. In one scene, he prays:

> **"GOD, FILL ME WITH COURAGE,** with power, with whatever I need to be a witness. I don't want to be afraid anymore. I don't want to wait any longer. I don't want to worry about offending. Give me a persuasiveness rooted in the truth of your Word. I know it is your Spirit that draws people, but use me. . . . Please, Lord. Help me."
> (*Left Behind,* p. 346)

17. How courageous and bold are you in talking to others about Christ? Why?

_____

_____

_____

_____

18. Why do you think some Christians seem to be able to discuss spiritual issues with such confidence and ease?

_____

_____

_____

_____

19. What would it take for you to be willing to pray what Rayford prayed?

_____

_____

_____

_____

Pursuing the Truth

Consider what the following Bible verses have to say about taking the initiative and being bold in witness:

Acts 1:8 (an angel speaking to first-generation Christians): *"But when the Holy Spirit has come upon you, you will receive power and will tell people about me everywhere—in Jerusalem, throughout Judea, in Samaria, and to the ends of the earth."*

Acts 4:29, 31 (the early church praying together): *" 'And now, O Lord, hear their threats, and give your servants great boldness in their preaching.'. . . After this prayer, the building where they were meeting shook, and they were all filled with the Holy Spirit. And they preached God's message with boldness."*

Colossians 4:3–4 (Paul writing to his Christian friends): *"Don't forget to pray for us, too, that God will give us many opportunities to preach. . . . Pray that I will proclaim this message as clearly as I should."*

20. What do these passages suggest is necessary for bold, successful witnessing?

_____

_____

_____

_____

_____

21. Some well-meaning Christians have been known to get so excited about the two-phased return of Christ and all the other prophetic passages of Scripture, that they have actually tried to predict the date of the Rapture. What do you think about this?

_____

_____

_____

_____

_____

"The Bible teaches us, 'Let your moderation be known unto all men' (Philippians 4:5, KJV). A study of 'signs' of the end of the age or the return of Christ should always be undertaken with a degree of restraint. Date-setters are to be ignored or, even better, rebuked as false teachers. It mystifies us that men would try to set dates for the return of Christ in view of the warning of our Lord himself: 'Of that day and hour no one knows, no, not even the angels of heaven, but my Father only.' (Matthew 24:36). 'It is not for you to know times or seasons which the Father has put in his own authority.' (Acts 1:7)

"Those two verses alone should warn us that anyone who suggests a date for the return of Christ is wrong. However, the Lord did say in the parable of the fig tree that we can know the general time of his coming. As Jesus said, 'So you also, when you see all these things, know that it is near, at the door' (Matthew 24:33)."[4]

Tim LaHaye and Jerry Jenkins

22. How will your prayer life change in response to the things you've studied in this lesson?

_____

_____

_____

_____

_____

23. What questions do you still have about the Rapture or the Second Coming?

_____

_____

_____

_____

_____

_____

Lesson in Review . . .

- The return of Christ has two phases or stages.
- The first phase is called the Rapture (the "blessed hope") and involves Christians being caught up into the air to be with Christ forever.
- The second stage is called the Glorious Appearing and involves Christ coming to earth to judge and rule for a thousand years.
- The two aspects of Christ's coming are separated by at least seven years, a period known as the Tribulation.
- In light of the surety of Christ's return, we should boldly tell others so they can be prepared.

The Rapture

Lesson 5
Aftermath

Where were you when . . .

- President Kennedy was shot?
- you heard the news about 9-11?
- the space shuttle *Columbia* broke apart?

1. In your opinion, how do these recent, terrible events compare to the national and international upheaval that will occur immediately following the Rapture?

   _____

   _____

   _____

   _____

   _____

   _____

Unfolding the Story
(*Left Behind*, pp. 46–47)

Like all great storytellers, the authors of *Left Behind* begin with a bang—the account of the jaw-dropping event the Bible calls "the blessed hope" and most people call "the Rapture." Immediately following this inexplicable disappearance of millions, pandemonium breaks loose. Those left behind find themselves in a weird "twilight zone" world, where everything has changed and nothing is certain. The authors depict the chaos well in this scene:

FINALLY IN THE TERMINAL, Rayford found crowds standing in lines behind banks of phones. Most had angry people waiting, yelling at callers who shrugged and redialed. Airport snack bars and restaurants were already sold out of or low on food, and all newspapers and magazines were gone. In shops where staffers had disappeared, looters walked off with merchandise. . . .

Rayford got in line, beginning to feel the tension of having flown too long and known too little. Worse was the knowledge that he had a better idea than most of what had happened. If he was right, if it were true, he would not be getting an answer when he dialed home. As he stood there, a TV monitor above him broadcast images of the chaos. From around the globe came wailing mothers, stoic families, reports of death and destruction. Dozens of stories included eyewitnesses who had seen their loved ones and friends disappear before their eyes.

Most shocking to Rayford was a woman in labor, about to go into the delivery room, who was suddenly barren. Doctors delivered the placenta. Her husband had caught the disappearance of the fetus on tape. As he videotaped her great belly and sweaty face, he asked questions. How did she feel? "How do you think I feel, Earl? Turn that thing off." What was she hoping for? "That you'll get close enough for me to slug you." Did she realize that in a few moments they'd be parents? "In about a minute, you're going to be divorced."

Then came the scream and the dropping of the camera, terrified voices, running nurses, and the doctor. CNN reran the footage in super slow motion, showing the woman going from very pregnant to nearly flat stomached, as if she had instantaneously delivered. "Now, watch with us again," the newsman intoned, "and keep your eyes on the left edge of your screen, where a nurse appears to be reading a printout from the fetal heart monitor. There, see?" The action stopped as the pregnant woman's stomach deflated. "The nurse's uniform seems to still be standing as if an invisible person is wearing it. She's gone. Half a second later, watch." The tape moved ahead and stopped. "The uniform, stockings and all, are in a pile atop her shoes."

Local television stations from around the world reported bizarre occurrences, especially in time zones where the event had happened during the day or early evening. CNN showed via satellite the video of a groom disappearing while slipping the ring onto his bride's finger. A funeral home in Australia reported that nearly every mourner disappeared from one memorial service, including the corpse, while at another service at the same time, only a few disappeared and the corpse remained. Morgues also reported corpse disappearances. At a burial, three of six pallbearers stumbled and dropped a casket when the other three disappeared. When they picked up the casket, it too was empty.

Rayford was second in line for the phone, but what he saw next on the screen convinced him he would never see his wife again. At a Christian high school soccer game at a missionary headquarters in Indonesia, most of the spectators and all but one of the players disappeared in the middle of play, leaving their shoes and uniforms on the ground. The CNN reporter announced that, in his remorse, the surviving player took his own life.

2. If you had to guess, what would you say were probably the top five or six emotions swirling about in Rayford's heart and mind in the scene above? Which one do you think would be your own strongest response in a similar situation?

_____

_____

_____

_____

_____

3. In several places, the authors portray people taking their own life in the aftermath of the Rapture. Why would anyone do this?

_____

_____

_____

_____

Back to Reality

Many read such an account, ponder such events, and think, *No. Surely not. Could such amazing things really take place?* They not only can—they *will! Left Behind* may be a work of fiction. But the events described in its exciting pages are real—revealed matter-of-factly in the pages of the Bible.

Many grapple with the thought of unmanned vehicles, runaway trains, missing salesclerks, army units decimated, top government positions suddenly unfilled, and conclude it's all too far-fetched, too preposterous for the modern mind. *This is the stuff of a sci-fi movie, not real life!*

And yet how could it be otherwise? If Christians are caught up suddenly to meet the Lord in the air, they will no longer be clothed, no longer be performing earthly tasks. Bodies of dead believers will be raised to be reunited with their souls. Life on earth will change more quickly and more radically than at any moment in human history. What a sobering thought!

4. Think through a list of common occupations, and try to imagine the practical impact of people and workers in those fields suddenly gone and no longer doing their jobs (military commanders, police, political leaders, etc.).

    _____

    _____

    _____

    _____

    _____

5. List some reactions and behaviors that would likely occur in your hometown if large numbers of people were suddenly missing.

    _____

    _____

    _____

    _____

    _____

Understanding the Word

The Bible gives us a number of fascinating clues as to what happens at and immediately following the Rapture. Let's look at the experiences, first for believers, and then for unbelievers.

The Aftermath for Believers

Read the following passages about what will be true for Christians at the moment of the Rapture.

But let me tell you a wonderful secret God has revealed to us. Not all of us will die, but we will all be transformed. It will happen in a moment, in the blinking of an eye, when the last trumpet is blown. For when the trumpet sounds, the Christians who have died will be raised with transformed bodies. And then we who are living will be transformed so that we will never die. For our perishable earthly bodies must be transformed into heavenly bodies that will never die. (1 Corinthians 15:51–53)

But we are citizens of heaven, where the Lord Jesus Christ lives. And we are eagerly waiting for him to return as our Savior. He will take these weak mortal bodies of ours and change them into glorious bodies like his own, using the same mighty power that he will use to conquer everything, everywhere. (Philippians 3:20–21)

6. What do these verses say will happen to our bodies?

    _____

    _____

    _____

    _____

    _____

7. What is a "heavenly body"? What clues about our future, glorified bodies do we get from studying the resurrected body of Jesus? (Hint: see Luke 24:36, 41–43.)

    _____

    _____

    _____

    _____

    _____

    _____

8. What do the following verses contribute to your understanding of the Christian's experience at and immediately following the Rapture?

    After all, what gives us hope and joy, and what is our proud reward and crown? It is you! Yes, you will bring us much joy as we stand together before our Lord Jesus when he comes back again. For you are our pride and joy. (1 Thessalonians 2:19–20)

> *Yes, dear friends, we are already God's children, and we can't even imagine what we will be like when Christ returns. But we do know that when he comes we will be like him, for we will see him as he really is.* (1 John 3:2)

> *And when the head Shepherd comes, your reward will be a never-ending share in his glory and honor.* (1 Peter 5:4)

_____

_____

_____

_____

_____

The Aftermath for Unbelievers

The apostle Paul had a special affection for the Thessalonian Christians. They had responded to the good news of Christ with joy and wholehearted commitment. In his short time with them, Paul had apparently given them a crash course in end-times theology. Yet almost immediately a group of false teachers had infiltrated the church and created confusion and fear by suggesting that the Second Coming had already occurred. In his letters to the church, Paul set about correcting these misconceptions. In his second letter to the church, Paul said:

> *Don't be fooled by what they say. For that day will not come until there is a great rebellion against God and the man of lawlessness is revealed—the one who brings destruction. He will exalt himself and defy every god there is and tear down every object of adoration and worship. He will position himself in the temple of God, claiming that he himself is God. Don't you remember that I told you this when I was with you? And you know what is holding him back, for he can be revealed only when his time comes.*

> *For this lawlessness is already at work secretly, and it will remain secret until the one who is holding it back steps out of the way.* (2 Thessalonians 2:3–7)

9. What, according to Paul, will have to happen before the "man of lawlessness" (i.e., the Antichrist) can be revealed?

_____

_____

_____

_____

_____

_____

10. Who is holding back or restraining the man of lawlessness?

_____

_____

_____

_____

"The Tribulation will not begin until the Antichrist . . . is revealed. And he won't be revealed until the restrainer, the Holy Spirit, is taken off the earth.

"Follow the reasoning here. The Holy Spirit dwells in the church. He came at Pentecost to take up his residence in the body of believers who make up the church. In fact, it is Holy Spirit baptism that marks a person as a member of Christ's body, the church (1 Corinthians 12:13).

"So if the Tribulation doesn't begin until the Antichrist is revealed, and if he won't be revealed until after the Holy Spirit leaves, guess who leaves when the Spirit leaves? The church!"[1]

Tony Evans

In the final letter he ever wrote, the apostle Paul was inspired to describe the decadent nature of earth's final days.

But mark this: There will be terrible times in the last days. People will be lovers of themselves, lovers of money, boastful, proud, abusive, disobedient to their parents, ungrateful, unholy, without love, unforgiving, slanderous, without self-control, brutal, not lovers of the good, treacherous, rash, conceited, lovers of pleasure rather than lovers of God—having a form of godliness but denying its power. Have nothing to do with them. (2 Timothy 3:1–5 NIV)

11. Can you give some present-day, specific examples of the sins listed by Paul? Have you seen them become more pronounced in your lifetime? If so, how exactly?

_____

_____

_____

_____

_____

_____

12. When you think of the degree to which these godless attitudes and actions are already present in the world, how much worse will conditions be with those called to be "salt and light" (see Matthew 5:13–14) gone from society?

_____

_____

_____

_____

Finding the Connection

(*Soul Harvest,* pp. 325–26)

In *Soul Harvest,* the fourth volume of the Left Behind series, a Jewish believer/Bible scholar named Tsion hosts an Internet bulletin board in which he can teach God's truth and warn earth's survivors of the dangers of the beast and the fatal error of unbelief.

In one disturbing posting, he describes the world of television after the Rapture has occurred and Christians are no longer around to stem the flood of immorality.

> **ON VIRTUALLY EVERY OTHER CHANNEL,** however, I saw—in that split second before the signal changed—final proof that society has reached rock-bottom.
>
> I am neither naive nor prudish. But I saw things today I never thought I would see. All restraint, all boundaries, all limits have been eradicated. It was a microcosm of the reason for the wrath of the Lamb. Sexuality and sensuality and nudity have been part of the industry for many years. But even those who used to justify these on the basis of freedom of expression or a stand against censorship at the very least made them available only to people who knew what they were choosing.
>
> Perhaps it is the very loss of the children that has caused us not to forget God but to acknowledge him in the worst possible way, by sticking out our tongues, raising our fists, and spitting in his face. To see not just simulated perversion but actual portrayals of every deadly sin listed in the Scriptures left us feeling unclean.
>
> My friend left the room. I wept. It is no surprise to me that many have turned against God. But to be exposed to the depths of the result of this abandonment of the

Creator is a depressing and sorrowful thing. Real violence, actual tortures and murders, is proudly advertised as available 24 hours a day on some channels. Sorcery, black magic, clairvoyance, fortune-telling, witchcraft, seances, and spell casting are offered as simple alternatives to anything normal, let alone positive.

13. In what ways is society already hinting at what it will become when the Holy Spirit (living in believers) is removed from the scene?

_____

_____

_____

_____

14. Perhaps you've heard the analogy of the frog in the kettle? If you throw a frog into a pot of hot water, the critter will hop out immediately. However, if you put that frog in a pot of cool water, place it on a stove, and slowly raise the heat, you can boil the frog alive and it will never know the difference. In what ways is the modern-day church like the frog in a kettle? Why do you think so many Christians are unconcerned about the direction of society or even their own lives?

_____

_____

_____

_____

_____

"A good understanding of prophecy can give us a reference point for living. When a farmer wants to plow a straight furrow, he picks out a marker at the other side of the field and keeps his eyes on it as he plows. You need a reference point when you are looking into the future. If you're just entering college and you want to be a doctor, that's your reference point. Your goal will determine what courses you take and the path you follow. You will most certainly set your sights on medical school.

"The Bible says if you fix your sights and your hope on Christ's coming, that perspective on tomorrow will keep you on the straight and narrow today. Prophecy can help us walk a straight line." [2]

Tony Evans

Making the Change

God's desire is not for educated sinners but consecrated saints. He gave us his Word, not for the purposes of *information* but for inward, personal, spiritual *transformation* to take place. Head knowledge isn't what God is after here. Life change is the point of these studies.

In the shocking aftermath of the Rapture, characters like Rayford Steele and Buck Williams were left behind to seek, discover, and apply the truth. Together they faced the difficult task of following Christ during the terrible time of the Tribulation.

Though we have the distinct advantage of being able to learn from their experiences, we still have choices to make. Are we going to follow Christ? What are we going to do *now*, so that we are ready *then?*

15. In addition to a better understanding of the biblical teaching about the end times, what can you do to prepare your heart for this eventual reality?

_____

_____

_____

_____

16. As you read in the novel(s), the Left Behind characters experienced a roller coaster of emotions and were forced to make a number of decisions. Why do you think some were more reluctant or more hesitant to make an "all-out" commitment to Christ?

_____

_____

_____

_____

17. As you look at your own life right now, are there attitudes or actions that are displeasing to God? What do you intend to do about these?

_____

_____

_____

_____

"We prefer to call this miraculous event 'the blessed hope,' the term Paul uses in Titus 2:13: 'Looking for the blessed hope and glorious appearing of our great God and Savior Jesus Christ.' That is exactly what the Rapture is, a blessed hope.

"When the Bible uses the word 'hope' here, it does not mean a nice thing we earnestly suspect might happen, but rather a certified fact of the future, promised by God's unfailing Word. In this case, 'hope' means a present, confident expectation of a certain event."[3]

Tim LaHaye and Jerry Jenkins

Pursuing the Truth

18. What would you say to the skeptical friend who called this whole study "a bunch of religious poppycock"?

_____

_____

_____

_____

_____

19. Revelation 9:20–21 describes the mind-set and actions of those on the earth after the Rapture:

But the people . . . still refused to turn from their evil deeds. They continued to worship demons and idols made of gold, silver, bronze, stone, and wood—idols that neither see nor hear nor walk! And they did not repent of their murders or their witchcraft or their immorality or their thefts.

How do you explain this? What would prompt such breathtaking stubbornness?

_____

_____

_____

_____

20. What is one specific change you want to make in your life as a result of this study?

_____

_____

_____

_____

Lesson in Review . . .

- The Rapture will be an unforgettable, earthshaking event.
- Christians (both alive and dead) will be caught up together to meet Christ in the air. Changed gloriously and instantly, we will be taken to heaven and rewarded.
- Unbelievers will find themselves in what will seem to be a "God-forsaken" world where evil flourishes. And while some will turn to Christ, the majority will continue to reject God's truth and love.

LEFT

BEHIND

The Rapture

Lesson 6
Don't Be Left Behind

1. What is the most fear you've ever felt? What were the circumstances and what finally happened?

_____

_____

_____

_____

_____

> "The Old Testament features more than a hundred prophecies regarding the coming of the Messiah to the earth. Through these prophecies we know that Jesus was truly the Messiah, for he fulfilled every one of them. That is also how believers can be so confident that he will return physically to the earth to set up his kingdom, because he promised he would—five times more frequently than he promised to come the first time! Since his first coming is a fact of history, we can be at least five times as certain that he will come the second time."[1]
>
> Tim LaHaye and Jerry Jenkins

Unfolding the Story
(*Left Behind*, pp. 101–04)

With his wife and son gone, suddenly "snatched up" by God into heaven in the mysterious event known as the Rapture, airline pilot Rayford Steele is left with his daughter Chloe and a few other acquaintances to sort through his feelings, his fears, and his future. Authors LaHaye and Jenkins describe Rayford's whirlwind of emotions:

> **HE WAS EXHAUSTED,** and yet he couldn't bring himself to go upstairs again. . . . He lumbered to the couch and lay down, a sob in his throat but no more tears to accompany it. . . . Rayford lay there grieving, knowing the television would be full of scenes he didn't want to see, dedicated around the clock to the tragedy and mayhem all over the world. And then it hit him. He sat up, staring out the window in the darkness. He owed it to Chloe not to fail her. He loved her and she was all he had left. He had to find out how they had missed everything Irene had been trying to tell them, why it had been so hard to accept and believe. Above all, he had to study, to learn, to be prepared for whatever happened next.
>
> If the disappearances were of God, if they had been his doing, was this the end of it? The Christians, the real believers, get taken away, and the rest are left to grieve and mourn and realize their error? Maybe so. Maybe that was the price. But then what happens when we die? he thought. If heaven is real, if the Rapture was a fact, what does that say about hell and judgment? Is that our fate? We go through this hell of regret and remorse, and then we literally go to hell, too?
>
> Irene had always talked of a loving God, but even God's love and mercy had to have limits. Had everyone who denied the truth pushed God to his limit? Was there no more mercy, no second chance? Maybe there wasn't, and if that was so, that was so.
>
> But if there were options, if there was still a way to find the truth and believe or accept or whatever it was Irene said one was supposed to, Rayford was going to find it. Would it mean admitting that he didn't know everything? That he had relied on himself and that now he felt stupid and weak and worthless? He could admit that. After a lifetime of achieving, of excelling, of being better than most and the best in most circles, he had been as humbled as was possible in one stroke.
>
> There was so much he didn't know, so much he didn't understand. But if the answers were still there, he would find them. He didn't know whom to ask or where to start, but this was something he and Chloe could do together. . . . They would be on a mission, a quest for truth. If he was already too late, he would have to accept and deal with that. He'd always been one who went for a goal and accepted the consequences. Only these consequences were eternal. He hoped against all hope that there was another chance at truth and knowledge out there somewhere. The only problem was that the ones who knew were gone.

2. Why does it often take a personal or national crisis before most people will ponder the deep spiritual realities of life?

_____

_____

_____

_____

_____

3. The opening pages make it clear that Rayford did not share his wife's enthusiasm for Christ. Why not? What are the most common problems faced by couples who do not see eye to eye on spiritual matters?

_____

_____

_____

_____

_____

Back to Reality

Rayford's dilemma is ours too. The only difference is chronological. By the time the novels begin, he has no more time to get ready, no choice but to react to each new development. He now faces the daunting task of trying to make sense of end-times events as they unfold in rapid-fire fashion around him. We, on the other hand, have the luxury of advance notice. We have time to prepare a wise response. And so we need to work to understand all these prophetic realities *before* the first domino falls.

4. Are you a procrastinator? Do you tend to put off important decisions and actions? What attitude do you think lies behind your procrastination?

_____

_____

_____

_____

5. If you were due to leave on a long trip within the week, what would you do to get ready? If you were having an "important" guest for dinner, what preparations would you make? Why?

    _____

    _____

    _____

    _____

    _____

    _____

    _____

    _____

6. To what degree do you think pride might play a part in the average person's stubborn refusal to get ready for the return of Christ?

    _____

    _____

    _____

    _____

    _____

Understanding the Word

Coming straight from the compassionate heart of God, the Bible is a medicine chest of help and hope for terminally ill people in a diseased and dying world. God's Word not only diagnoses our spiritual condition; it also prescribes a solution.

First, it warns us of our condition—the folly of pride:

The Lord despises pride; be assured that the proud will be punished. (Proverbs 16:5)

Pride goes before destruction, and haughtiness before a fall. (Proverbs 16:18)

Pride ends in humiliation, while humility brings honor. (Proverbs 29:23)

In addition, the prophetic books that look ahead to the events surrounding the return of Christ repeat over and over sentiments like this:

> *In that day the arrogant will be brought down to the dust; the proud will be humbled.* (Isaiah 5:15)

7. According to the Scriptures, why does God hate pride so much?

    _____

    _____

    _____

    _____

    _____

    _____

8. How would you define pride? What does it look like in a person who is disinterested in God?

    _____

    _____

    _____

    _____

    _____

    _____

British author C. S. Lewis, in his masterpiece *Mere Christianity,* calls pride "The Great Sin" and devotes an entire chapter to the subject. He observes:

"It was through Pride that the devil became the devil. Pride leads to every other vice: it is the complete anti-God state of mind. . . . In God you come up against something which is in every respect immeasurably superior to yourself. Unless you know God as that—and therefore, know yourself as nothing in comparison—you do not know God at all. As long as you are proud you cannot know God. A proud man is always looking down on things and people, and, of course, as long as you are looking down, you cannot see something that is above you." [2]

Second, the Bible reveals the fierce desire of God to save us from sin and eternal death (and also his infinite patience with prideful people):

> For God so loved the world that he gave his only Son, so that everyone who believes in him will not perish but have eternal life. (John 3:16)

> God our Savior . . . wants everyone to be saved and to understand the truth. (1 Timothy 2:3–4)

> The Lord isn't really being slow about his promise to return, as some people think. No, he is being patient for your sake. He does not want anyone to perish, so he is giving more time for everyone to repent. (2 Peter 3:9)

9. What do these verses reveal about God's heart? Do these insights "fit" with what you have formerly believed about God?

_____

_____

_____

_____

_____

Third, the Bible declares what we must do in order to have our sin and pride forgiven and cleansed. It shows how we can be brought back into a right relationship with God:

> But to all who believed him [Jesus] and accepted him, he gave the right to become children of God. (John 1:12)

> He is so rich in kindness that he purchased our freedom through the blood of his Son, and our sins are forgiven. (Ephesians 1:7)

> God saved you by his special favor when you believed. And you can't take credit for this; it is a gift from God. Salvation is not a reward for the good things we have done, so none of us can boast about it. (Ephesians 2:8–9)

10. What do these verses teach about how to become a child of God?

_____

_____

_____

_____

_____

_____

11. According to these verses, are we saved from sin and forgiven by God on the basis of something we do? How do you know?

_____

_____

_____

_____

_____

_____

Finding the Connection

Buck Williams, senior writer for *Global Weekly,* is one of the main characters in the Left Behind series. When we first meet him, he is a very self-assured "man of the world." All through the first novel, he is irreligious and secular in his thinking. Initially, the sudden disappearance of millions from the earth is nothing more than a great story, the scoop of a lifetime. And yet supernatural events slowly but surely force Buck to reckon with the deepest questions of life. Is there a God? Is the Bible true? What do I do with the claims of Christ?

As he meets others who have been left behind and hears them powerfully articulate how these earth-shattering events are foretold in the Bible, he has a huge choice to make. It is a painful decision for Buck, just as it is for people today. In order for Buck to acknowledge the reality of God and the truth of his Word, he will have to let go of his professional and intellectual pride and humble himself. He will have to admit his previous ideas and way of life were wrong and embrace the claims of Christ and trust in someone other than himself.

12. Why is it so hard to humble ourselves, to admit that we need help, that we are weak, or that we don't know?

_____

_____

_____

_____

_____

_____

James 4:6 says:

> As the Scriptures say, "God sets himself against the proud, but he shows favor to the humble."

13. What are some ways the humble are shown favor? Where have you found this principle to be true in your life?

_____

_____

_____

_____

_____

Making the Change

(*Left Behind*, 441–42, 446–47)

All of Scripture, inspired by God, speaks change into our lives. The Gospels that tell of Jesus' life, the letters that give so much direction to believers, the historic books that remind of God's great works in the past, and the prophetic writings that unfold God's plan for the world all challenge us to change. God's Word makes us just as accountable as it makes the characters in the Left Behind series.

BUCK'S CAREER BROUGHT HIM IN CONTACT with many people whose lives were transformed to the likeness of Jesus Christ. He watched as friends and coworkers committed themselves to God, and they encouraged him to do the same. Buck, being the analytical type, took his time to evaluate the implications of a decision for Christ. . . .

All the way to the United Nations [Buck] agonized. Do I "pray the prayer" as so many of those people said yesterday morning? . . . He decided that becoming a believer could not be for the purpose of having a good luck charm. That would cheapen it. Surely God didn't work that way. . . . There was only reason to make the transaction, he decided—if he truly believed he could be forgiven and become one of God's people. God had become more than a force of nature or even a miracle worker to Buck, as God had been in the skies of Israel that night. It only made sense that if God made people, he would want to communicate with them, to connect with them. . . .

"God," he said, "I need you, and not just for this meeting." And as he prayed, he believed. This was no experiment, no halfhearted attempt. He wasn't just hoping or trying something out. Buck knew that he was talking to God himself. He admitted that he needed God, that he knew he was as lost and as sinful as anyone. He didn't specifically pray the prayer he had heard others talk about, but when he finished, he had covered the same territory and the deal was done. Buck was not the type to go into anything lightly. As well as he knew anything, he knew there would be no turning back.

14. How did Buck's heart change?

_____

_____

_____

_____

_____

15. How did he deal with the barriers that had hindered his belief?

_____

_____

_____

_____

_____

16. Have you ever made this type of commitment to God? What happened as a result?

_____

_____

_____

_____

_____

_____

17. If you haven't, what is keeping you from trusting Christ right now?

_____

_____

_____

_____

_____

_____

Pursuing the Truth

If you have already put your faith in Christ (or if you just did), you now have the obligation to live in light of his coming. Consider these passages, written to believers, that give us a "job description" in these "last days":

> For the grace of God has been revealed, bringing salvation to all people. And we are instructed to turn from godless living and sinful pleasures. We should live in this evil world with self-control, right conduct, and devotion to God, while we look forward to that wonderful event when the glory of our great God and Savior, Jesus Christ, will be revealed. He gave his life to free us from every kind of sin, to cleanse us, and to make us his very own people, totally committed to doing what is right. (Titus 2:11–14)

> And now, dear children, continue to live in fellowship with Christ so that when he returns, you will be full of courage and not shrink back from him in shame. Since we know that God is always right, we also know that all who do what is right are his children.
>
> See how very much our heavenly Father loves us, for he allows us to be called his children, and we really are! But the people who belong to this world don't know God, so they don't understand that we are his children. Yes, dear friends, we are already God's children, and we can't even imagine what we will be like when Christ returns. But we do know that when he comes we will be like him, for we will see him as he really is. And all who believe this will keep themselves pure, just as Christ is pure. (1 John 2:28–3:3)

18. How are Christians instructed to live in light of the imminent return of Christ?

_____

_____

_____

_____

_____

_____

19. What is "fellowship with Christ" and why is it so important?

_____

_____

_____

_____

_____

20. What are the potential consequences for believers who do not keep themselves pure?

_____

_____

_____

_____

_____

In the book *Prophecy in Light of Today*, Dr. Larry Mercer reminds us of the importance of remembering that God *does* have a plan for human history. He says that studying and understanding God's prophetic plan:

- helps us understand how to live today
- reminds us that this present earth is not our final home
- helps us keep our hearts turned toward eternity rather than being distracted by the trappings of time
- helps us guard against becoming too complacent and comfortable in this life
- keeps us from being surprised by evil
- motivates us to be light-bearers[3]

Authors Tim LaHaye and Jerry Jenkins sound a similar note in their companion book to the Left Behind novels, *Are We Living in the End Times?*:

> *Properly taught, prophecy emphasizes the "imminent" return of Christ—that he could come at any moment. This has proven to be one of the most spiritually motivating forces in church history. For whether it is the church of the first three centuries or that of the last two centuries, prophecy has had three effects on the church:*
> - *It has challenged believers to holy living in an unholy age;*
> - *It has given Christians a greater challenge to evangelize; and*
> - *It has caused the church to be more missionary minded as the church has realized it must fulfill the great commission before Christ returns.*[4]

Tony Evans adds a challenging word to those who might minimize the role of prophecy in a believer's life:

> *God does not tell us about the future so we can argue about it or show how much we know. He wants us to know the truth about tomorrow and about eternity, because people on their way to hell need to know God today, before it's too late for them.*[5]

A Personal Experience
TOP TEN LIST

God has put the following ten people (family members, friends, neighbors, classmates, work associates, etc.) on my heart. I am concerned about their spiritual well-being—about whether they know Christ, about whether they realize that his return is soon.

    I commit to pray for them—for God to draw them to himself, for Christ to make himself real to them, and for the Spirit of God to open their eyes to the truth of the gospel. I also commit to spend time with these loved ones and to be ready to make a defense to everyone who asks me to give an account for the hope that is in me (see 1 Peter 3:15).

1. _____
2. _____
3. _____
4. _____
5. _____
6. _____

7. _____

8. _____

9. _____

10. _____

"The rapture is the hope of the church. . . . If our Lord had planned that we endure part or all of the Tribulation we would accept that as his will. If he promises to remove us from that awful time, we thank him most gratefully. But whatever view we hold, we know that when he appears, we shall be like him—pure, without sin, and righteous (1 John 3:2–7). Therefore every day until we die or are raptured, we should continually be purifying our lives (1 John 3:3), be abounding in the work of the Lord (1 Corinthians 15:58), and be loving his appearing (2 Timothy 4:8).

"He says, 'I am coming quickly.' We say, 'Come, Lord Jesus' " (Revelation 22:20).[6]

Charles Ryrie

First Corinthians 1:7–9 says:

Now you have every spiritual gift you need as you eagerly wait for the return of our Lord Jesus Christ. He will keep you strong right up to the end, and he will keep you free from all blame on the great day when our Lord Jesus Christ returns. God will surely do this for you, for he always does just what he says, and he is the one who invited you into this wonderful friendship with his Son, Jesus Christ our Lord.

21. What has God provided his children as they wait for Christ? How can we be sure of this? (Hint: see verse 7.)

_____

_____

_____

22. What should be our attitude as we wait for "the blessed hope"?

_____

_____

_____

Authors LaHaye and Jenkins conclude their book *Are We Living in the End Times?* in this fashion:

The story is told of a little girl who had trouble sleeping one night. Her bedroom was upstairs, and her parents were downstairs reading. First she asked for a glass of water, then a cookie, and then she wanted to know what time it was. Finally her parents' patience ran out, and they warned her to go to sleep, threatening to punish her if she called them again.

The best she could do was lie there, watching the ceiling and listening for the striking of the grandfather clock downstairs. When the clock struck eleven, something must have gone wrong mechanically, because as she counted the hours, the clock tolled eleven and kept on going: twelve, thirteen, fourteen. When the clock tolled eighteen, she threw caution to the wind, jumped out of bed, ran downstairs, and cried, "Mom, Dad—it's later than it's ever been!"

That is what we are saying to you—prophetically, it is later than it has ever been. We pray that you will live every day as though Jesus could come at any moment, because no generation of Christians ever had more reason for believing he could come in their lifetime than does ours![7]

Lesson in Review . . .

- The return of Christ is imminent; it could happen at any moment!
- Those who have not yet put their faith in Christ need to humble themselves and receive his free gift of salvation (i.e., forgiveness and new, eternal life).
- Those who already know Christ need to live expectantly—with holiness and boldness, telling everyone the good news that Jesus Christ is Savior and Lord, and that he is coming soon!

Endnotes

Lesson 1: Early Edition (How Biblical Prophecy Works)

1. Howard Hendricks, *Living by the Book* (Chicago: Moody, 1991), 17.
2. Charles Ryrie, *What You Should Know About the Rapture* (Chicago: Moody, 1981), 20–21.
3. John Walvoord, *The Prophecy Knowledge Handbook* (Wheaton: Dallas Seminary Press/Scripture Press, 1991), 10.

Lesson 2: Instant Exit

1. Charles Ryrie, *What You Should Know About the Rapture* (Chicago: Moody, 1991), 27–28.
2. John Walvoord, *The Prophecy Knowledge Handbook* (Wheaton: Dallas Seminary Press/Scripture Press, 1991), 484.
3. Tony Evans, *The Best Is Yet to Come* (Chicago: Moody, 2000), 16.
4. Ryrie, *What You Should Know*, 29.
5. Evans, *The Best Is Yet to Come*, 149.
6. Adapted from Tim LaHaye and Jerry B. Jenkins, *Are We Living in the End Times?* (Wheaton: Tyndale House, 1999), 101–2.

Lesson 3: The Big Picture

1. Tim LaHaye and Jerry B. Jenkins, *Are We Living in the End Times?* (Wheaton: Tyndale House, 1999), 71.
2. Charles H. Dyer, *World News and Bible Prophecy* (Wheaton: Tyndale House, 1993), 214–15.
3. LaHaye and Jenkins, *Are We Living in the End Times?* 151.
4. J. Dwight Pentecost, "The Glorious Appearing of Christ," in *Tim LaHaye Prophecy Study Bible* (Chattanooga: AMG Publishers, 2000), 1065.
5. LaHaye and Jenkins, *Are We Living in the End Times?* 252–53.
6. Ibid., 25–26.
7. Ibid., 8–9.
8. Tony Evans, *The Best Is Yet to Come* (Chicago: Moody, 2000), 31–32.

Lesson 4: One Coming—Two Phases

1. Tony Evans, *The Best Is Yet to Come* (Chicago: Moody, 2000), 15.
2. Tim LaHaye and Jerry B. Jenkins, *Are We Living in the End Times?* (Wheaton: Tyndale House, 1999), 98, 100, 104.
3. Howard Hendricks, *Living by the Book* (Chicago: Moody, 1991), 196–97.
4. LaHaye and Jenkins, *Are We Living in the End Times?* 22–23.

Lesson 5: Aftermath

1. Tony Evans, *The Best Is Yet to Come* (Chicago: Moody, 2000), 148.
2. Ibid., 23–24.
3. Tim LaHaye and Jerry B. Jenkins, *Are We Living in the End Times?* (Wheaton: Tyndale House, 1999), 98.

Lesson 6: Don't Be Left Behind

1. Tim LaHaye and Jerry B. Jenkins, *Are We Living in the End Times?* (Wheaton: Tyndale House, 1999), 3.
2. C. S. Lewis, *Mere Christianity* (New York: Collier Books/MacMillan, 1952), 94, 96.
3. Larry Mercer quoted in *Prophecy in Light of Today*, ed. Charles Dyer (Chicago: Moody, 2002), 117–22.
4. LaHaye and Jenkins, *Are We Living in the End Times?* 6–7.
5. Tony Evans, *The Best Is Yet to Come* (Chicago: Moody, 2000), 28–29.
6. Charles Ryrie, *Come Quickly, Lord Jesus* (Eugene, Ore.: Harvest House, 1996), 138–39.
7. LaHaye and Jenkins, *Are We Living in the End Times?* 364–65.

SINCE 1894, Moody Publishers has been dedicated to equip and motivate people to advance the cause of Christ by publishing evangelical Christian literature and other media for all ages, around the world. Because we are a ministry of the Moody Bible Institute of Chicago, a portion of the proceeds from the sale of this book go to train the next generation of Christian leaders.

If we may serve you in any way in your spiritual journey toward understanding Christ and the Christian life, please contact us at www.moodypublishers.com.

"All Scripture is God-breathed and is useful for teaching, rebuking, correcting and training in righteousness, so that the man of God may be thoroughly equipped for every good work."
—2 TIMOTHY 3:16, 17